Mel Bay's
Anthology of
Mandolin Music

By Bud Orr

THE AUTHOR

Eugene "Bud" Orr—Performing musician and teacher for the past 22 years at the "Neil Griffin Studios" located in Charlotte, North Carolina.

INTRODUCTION

In my teaching experience with mandolin students I find a very wide variety of musical tastes. Some prefer old time country, bluegrass, fiddle type tunes, country and western, international, popular and jazz. Today many young aspiring mandolin enthusiasts are enjoying rock and blues. Whatever your musical tastes, it is my sincere wish that this book contains something for everyone interested in the mandolin and it's music.

This book contains tablature making it possible to play without an understanding of musical notation. When playing the selections please pay more attention to the musical notation and use the tablature (Tab) more as an aid. By consistently doing this one will soon be able to play from books containing only the notes.

In some instances tablature is a great help in finding notes that can be played in several different places on the fingerboard.

Bud Orr

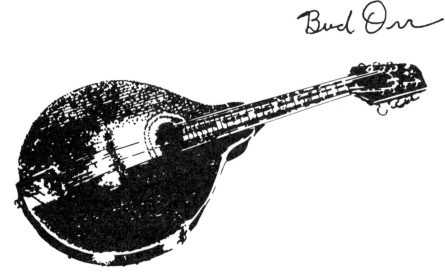

A BRIEF HISTORY OF THE MANDOLIN

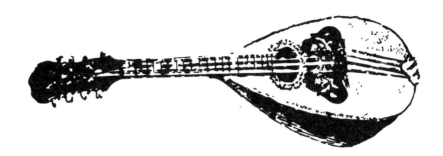

The mandolin is the newest and smallest member of the lute family of musical instruments and a distant relative of the mandola. In past centuries it has also been referred to as the mandora, mandore and mandolute. Many musicians and instrument builders were constantly experimenting, changing the shapes, names and tunings of these instruments. The final version was developed in Naples, Italy in 1790. The original Neapolitan mandolins retained the gourd—shaped back of the mandora with five double courses of ten strings.

Today's modern version of the mandolin consists of eight strings divided into four pairs and each pair is tuned in unison. The tuning is in major fifths like that of a violin making it very adaptable for playing from violin music.

Through the centuries many composers and musicians have made great contributions to the mandolin and its music. Among the best known are; Ludwig Van Beethoven, Antonio Vivaldi, Johann Adolph Hasse, Johann Conrad Schlick and Johann Neponuk Hummell. This time period ranged from 1759 until 1837. From 1863 until 1934 two brothers, Raffaele and Niccolo Calace contributed very much to the mandolin. Both were born in Naples, Italy sons of a stringed instrument maker. They received their musical education in Naples Conservatoire Of Music. Niccolo published about one hundred compositions for mandolin and piano. Raffaele contributed almost two hundred. The use of the mandolin in masterworks by Mozart shows the expressive powers of the instrument.

In 1898 Dave Apollon was born in Kiev Russia. He was the first to exploit and popularize the flat back mandolins being developed in the United States by large instrument manufacturing companies. His recording career from 1932 until shortly before his death in 1972 included many popular American standard songs and his playing was completely flawless. Dave Apollon will certainly be written in history as the "Greatest mandolin Virtuoso" of all times.

Howard Frye is a foremost performer of classical mandolin but does not limit himself to classical works. He has also recorded and performed haunting melodies of Gypsy music well suited for the instrument. The early sounds of country music growing into national prominence with what we know today as bluegrass music contained the sounds of the mandolin. The brother duets of the Monroe Brothers, the Blue Sky Boys and many others from the 1930's and 1940's. Today the instrument is heard in virtually every bluegrass band, both as a lead and rhythm instrument. From the wailing, bluesy bluegrass sounds of Bill Monroe, "The Father of Bluegrass" to the jazz of the all time great, Jethro Burns and the modern "Dawg" music of David Grisman, the mandolin today is enjoying more success than ever before in its history.

THE MANDOLIN AND ITS PARTS

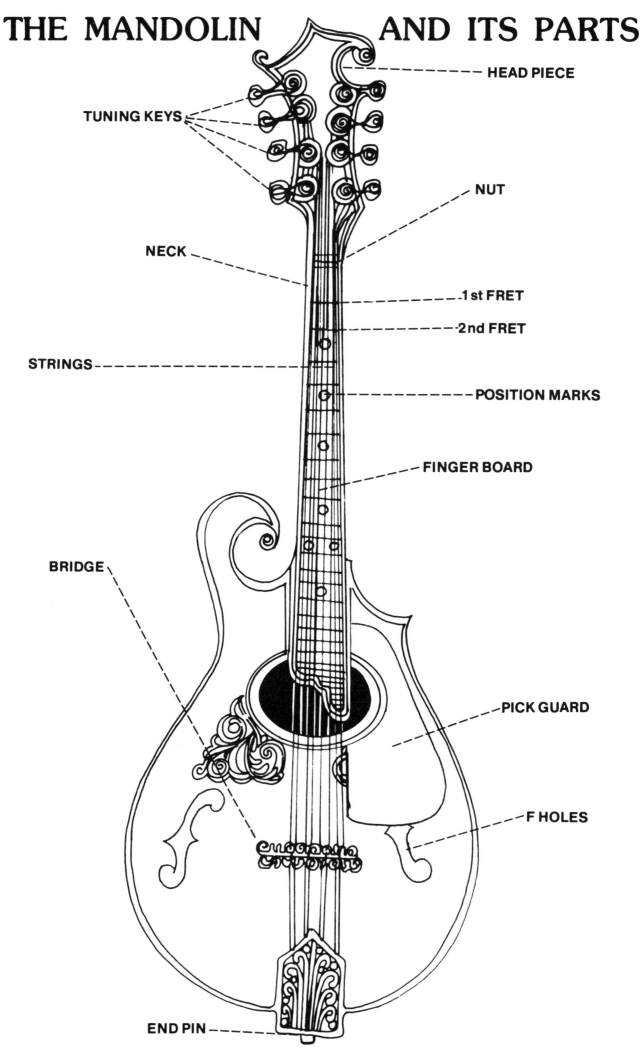

HEAD PIECE

TUNING KEYS

NUT

NECK

1st FRET

2nd FRET

STRINGS

POSITION MARKS

FINGER BOARD

BRIDGE

PICK GUARD

F HOLES

END PIN

4

HOLDING THE MANDOLIN

THE RIGHT HAND

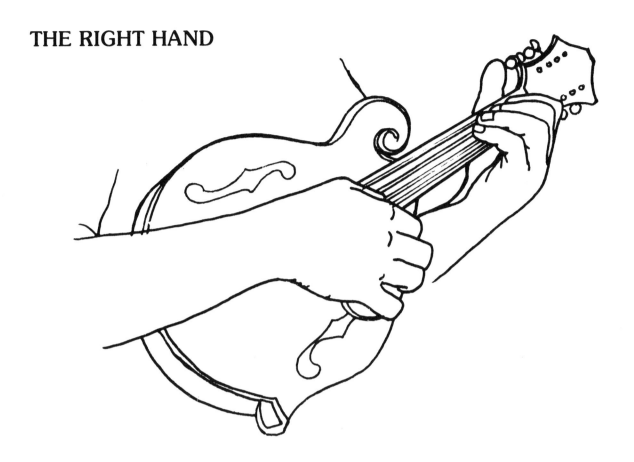

THE LEFT HAND

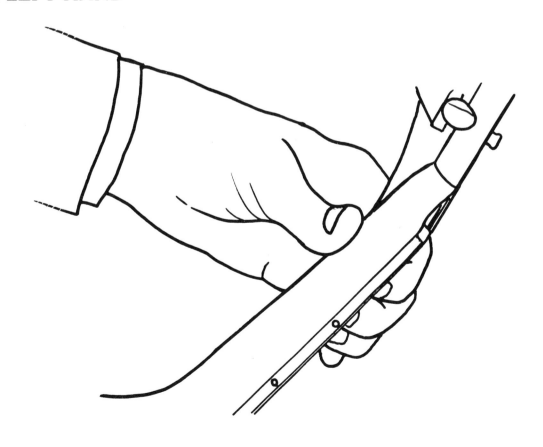

TUNING THE MANDOLIN

The mandolin is tuned like the violin. The first string E, second string A, third string D, fourth string G. (See diagram below for tuning) A pitch pipe for the violin may be purchased from any music store. The mandolin has duplicate strings for each pitch. These duplicate strings are tuned in unison.

1ST. STRING "E"	3RD. STRING "D"
2ND. STRING "A"	4TH. STRING "G"

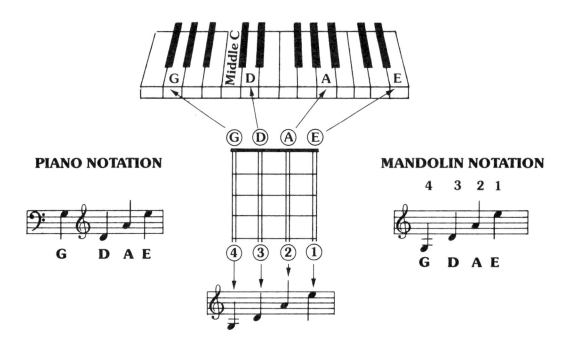

PIANO NOTATION

G   D   A   E

MANDOLIN NOTATION

4   3 2 1

G   D A E

ANOTHER METHOD OF TUNING

Place the finger behind the seventh fret of the fourth string to obtain the pitch of the third string (D).

Place the finger behind the seventh fret of the third string to obtain the pitch of the second string (A).

Place the finger behind the seventh fret of the second string to obtain the pitch of the first string (E).

PITCH PIPES

Pitch pipes for the mandolin (violin) may be purchased at any music store. Each pipe will have the correct pitch.

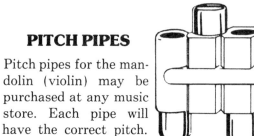

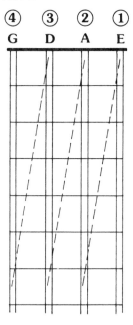

④ ③ ② ①

G   D   A   E

MUSIC READING SECTION

This section includes the following:

THE RUDIMENTS OF MUSIC
READING TABLATURE
MUSICAL SIGNS AND TERMS
1st and 2nd ENDINGS
TIME VALUES OF NOTES AND RESTS
TIME SIGNATURES
COUNTING TIME
COUNTING TIME IN TABLATURE
THE CYCLE OF KEYS
MANDOLIN FINGERBOARD CHART
MAJOR SCALES
SCALE AND TRANSPOSITION CHART
THE TREMOLO
DOUBLE NOTE STUDY
SCALE EXERCISES

THE RUDIMENTS OF MUSIC

Music is written on a staff consisting of five lines and four spaces as shown below.

Lines   Spaces

The lines and spaces are named after the first seven letters of the alphabet.

The five lines are named as follows:

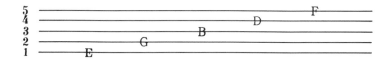

These letters can be remembered by this sentence:

<u>E</u>very <u>G</u>ood <u>B</u>oy <u>D</u>oes <u>F</u>ine.

The spaces are named as follows:

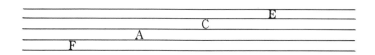

These letters can be remembered by spelling the word FACE.

The Treble or G Clef

Treble or G Clef sign   Bar line   Bar line

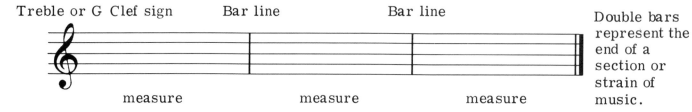

Double bars represent the end of a section or strain of music.

measure   measure   measure

READING TABLATURE

The mandolin consists of eight strings with each pair tuned in unison.

In Tablature only one line is used to represent both strings.

Tablature is simply a drawing of four lines to represent these strings. Numbers are given to show the musician that he is to either pick the open strings or in which fret he is to press the string down in order to produce the required note.

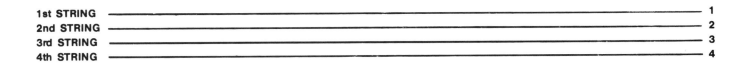

The numbers placed on the tablature lines show which fret to press down with the left hand fingers.

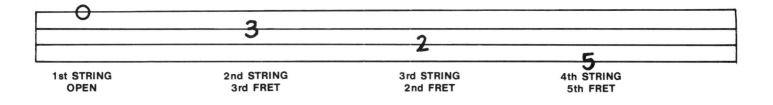

When two or more notes are to be played at the same time, they are shown as follows:

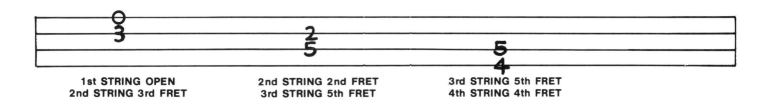

In this book all top notes are melody notes. If you experience difficulty at first in playing both notes, you should simply play the top note.

Musical Signs and Terms

Repeat Signs

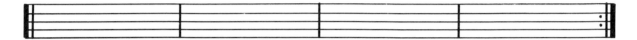

The two dots are called repeat signs. When there is only one set of dots, repeat from the beginning.

This means to repeat everything between the two sets of dots.

Repeat signs do not always mean to repeat from the beginning. They may also appear at any given place within the music.

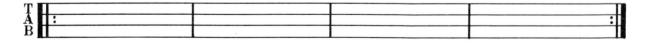

Repeat signs in tablature are written the same as in musical notation.

1st and 2nd Endings

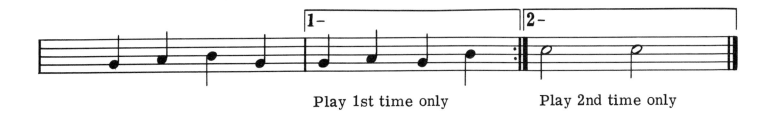

Play 1st time only   Play 2nd time only

Incomplete Measures

The example above shows two incomplete measures. Since we are playing in $\frac{4}{4}$ time, there should be 4 counts in each measure. The two notes in the first measure are called pick up notes, and the missing 2 counts are found in the last measure. The pick up notes in the first measure would be played alone with the mandolin and the down beat for the rhythm would begin in the second measure. If you play the song two or more times, the timing works out correctly.

TIME VALUES OF NOTES AND RESTS

For every note there is an equivalent rest sign.

The shape of a note tells how long it should sound before playing the next note.

A rest is not a note but a signature representing

a pause within the compass of a measure.

A dot placed after a note or rest increases it's original value by one half.

Here is a chart showing notes and rests and their relationship.

Notation	Name	Value	Rest Equivalent
𝅝	Whole Note	4 Counts	𝄻
𝅗𝅥.	Dotted Half Note	3 Counts	𝄼.
𝅗𝅥	Half Note	2 Counts	𝄼
𝅘𝅥	Quarter Note	1 Count	𝄽
𝅘𝅥𝅮	Eighth Note	1/2 Count	𝄾
𝅘𝅥𝅯	Sixteenth Note	1/4 Count	𝄿

Two notes of the same pitch are often tied together with a curved line meaning that one note equals the total value of both. Sound the note one time only and hold for the value of the two notes.

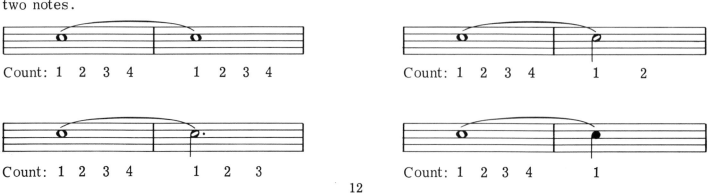

Count: 1 2 3 4   1 2 3 4   Count: 1 2 3 4   1   2

Count: 1 2 3 4   1 2 3   Count: 1 2 3 4   1

12

TIME SIGNATURES

The two numbers shown at the beginning of each piece of music are called time signatures. They show the total number of counts in each measure, and the type of note that receives one count. The top number gives the total number of counts in each measure. The bottom number gives the kind of note that receives one count. Keeping the correct time is just as important as playing the correct note. Strive to keep a steady and even beat from the beginning. Start out very slowly and speed will come with lots of practice.

Examples:

Four counts for each measure.

A quarter note receives one count.

Three counts for each measure.

A quarter note receives one count.

Two counts per measure.

A quarter note receives one count.

Counting Time
Counting in 4/4 Time

All notes that are 1 complete count or longer are picked down (⊓). Eighth notes are picked down (⊓) on the 1st half of a count and up (∨) on the last half.

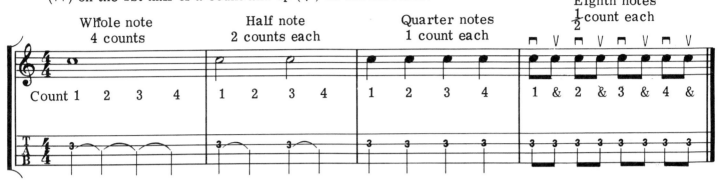

Counting in 3/4 Time

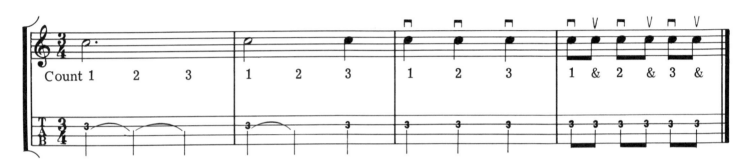

Counting in 2/4 Time

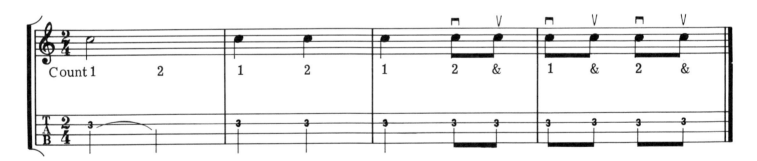

Counting with Tied and Dotted Notes

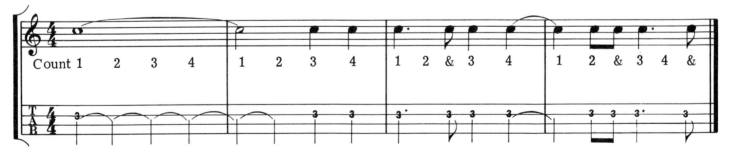

Picking symbols will not be shown in this book. You should observe the rules shown on this page.

Counting Time in Tablature

Counting time in tablature is exactly the same as in regular musical notation using the time signature at the beginning of the music. Measures are seperated by bar lines, with stems being used to indicate the different time values.

The only difference in tablature counting is when a note is to be held longer than one count. The first note will have the regular quarter note stem and will be connected with the lines to each additional quarter note being held.

Hold 4 counts   Hold 3 counts   Hold 2 counts

Dotted quarter notes are written in tablature and counted the same as in regular musical notation.

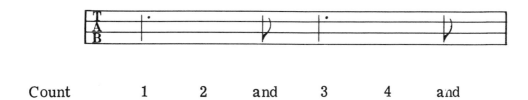

Count   1   2   and   3   4   and

15

THE CYCLE OF KEYS

Key signatures are shown below in the cycle of keys. Moving clockwise in scale 5ths are shown. Counter clockwise in scale 4ths are shown. The three main chords in any given key may be located as follows;

    1 - Find the name of the key in the circle below.
    2 - This will be the name of the main chord.
    3 - The two remaining chords are shown on each side.
    4 - Example :
        In the key of C major, C is the main chord.
        The two remaining chords would be F and G7.
    5 - Only the letter name of the chord is changed.
        7ths remain 7ths, Minors remain Minors, etc.

ENHARMONIC KEYS

Enharmonic keys sound the same but are written differently in musical notation.

Notice in the circle below the enharmonic keys overlap each other.

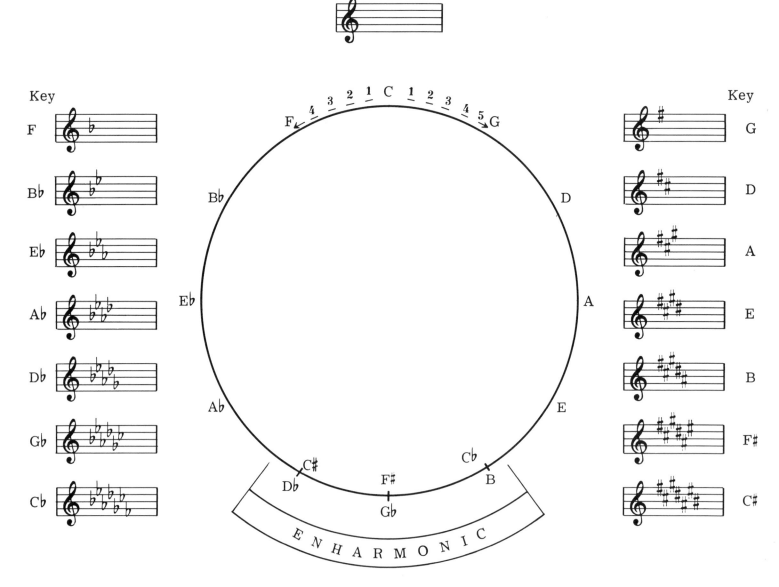

16

MANDOLIN FINGERBOARD CHART
(Showing All Of The Chromatic Notes)

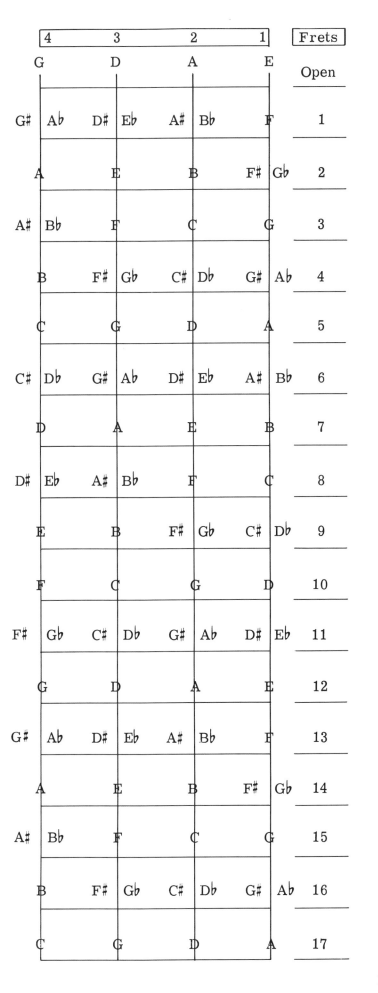

17

MAJOR SCALES
Practice Going Up and Back Down

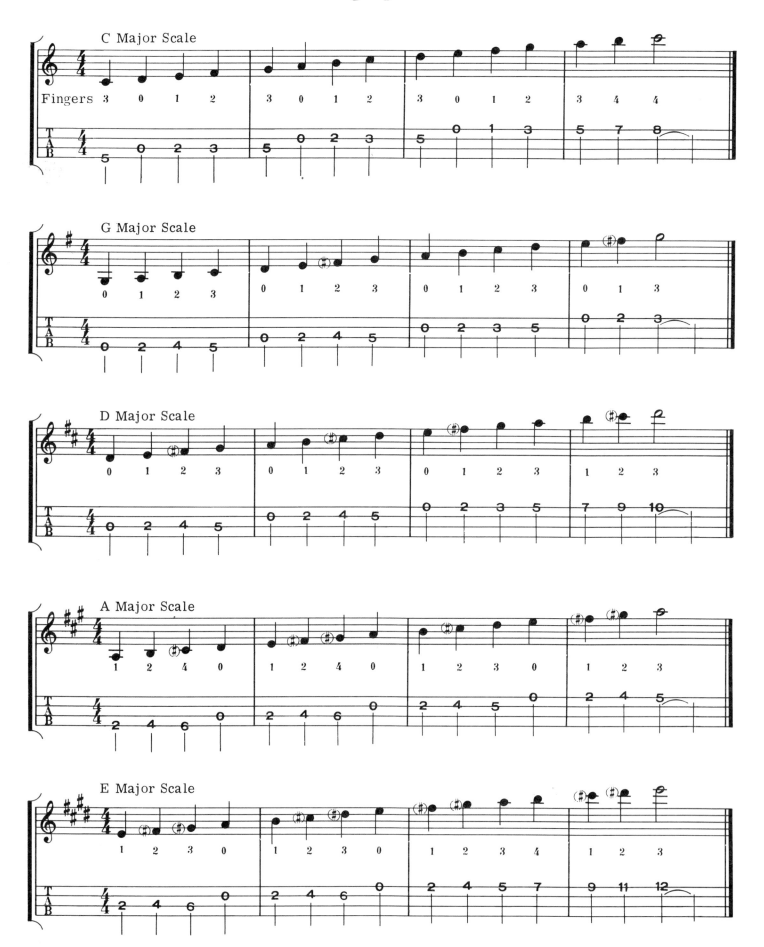

F Major Scale
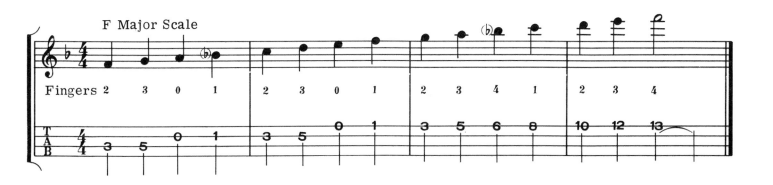

Bb Major Scale
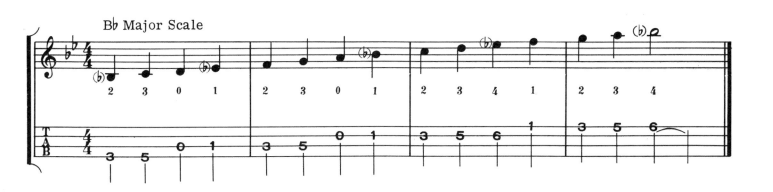

Eb Major Scale
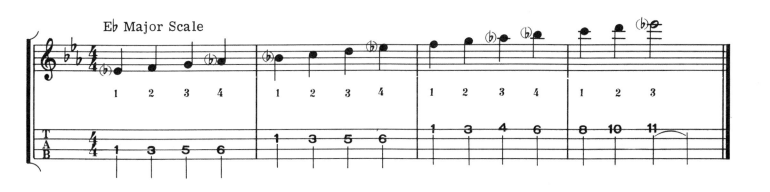

Ab Major Scale
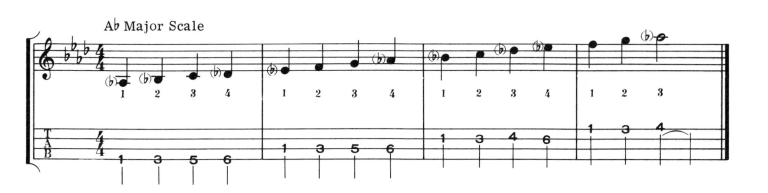

ENHARMONIC MAJOR SCALES

Enharmonic scales sound the same but are written differently in music notation. These three sets of scales will be studied together. The tablature shows that each set is played in the same position.

MOVABLE MAJOR SCALES

Ab major scale (2 octaves)

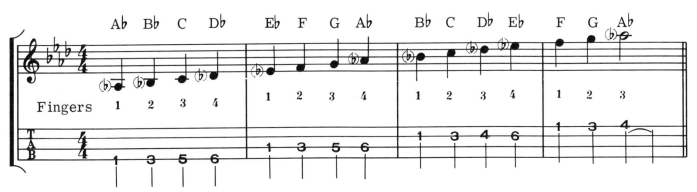

Sequence of notes

1	5	9	13
2	6	10	14
		11	15
3	7		
4	8	12	

Fret	Key
1	G# or Ab
2	A
3	A# or Bb
4	B
5	C
6	C# or Db
7	D
8	D# or Eb
9	E
10	F
11	F# or Gb
12	G

Fingers

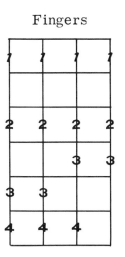

MOVABLE Bb MAJOR SCALE
1st And 2nd Strings
(One Octave)

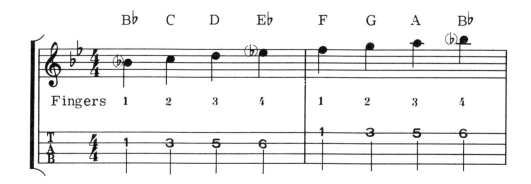

Sequence of notes		Fret	Key		Fingers

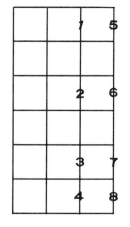

Fret	Key
1	A# or Bb
2	B
3	C
4	C# or Db
5	D
6	D# or Eb
7	E
8	F
9	F# or Gb
10	G
11	G# or Ab
12	A

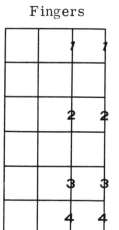

MOVABLE E♭ MAJOR SCALES
2nd And 3rd Strings
(One Octave)

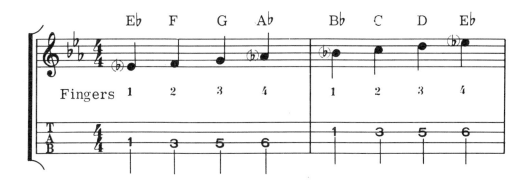

Sequence of notes	Fret	Key	Fingers
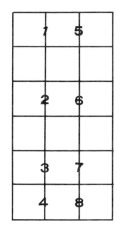	1	D♯ or E♭	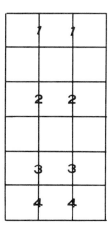
	2	E	
	3	F	
	4	F♯ or G♭	
	5	G	
	6	G♯ or A♭	
	7	A	
	8	A♯ or B♭	
	9	B	
	10	C	
	11	C♯ or D♭	
	12	D	

SCALE AND TRANSPOSITION CHART

The chart shown below may be used for notes or chords in changing from any given key to a different one.

To transpose first find the key in the first column at the left showing the key you are presently in.

Find the name of the key you are changing to moving up or down.

Moving from left to right shows the correct scale tones.

In transposing chords only the letter name is changed. The chord title, Minor, 7th, etc. remains the same as the origional.

Scale tones	1	2	3	4	5	6	7	8
Key								
C major No sharps No flats	C	D	E	F	G	A	B	C
G major 1 sharp	G	A	B	C	D	E	F♯	G
D major 2 sharps	D	E	F♯	G	A	B	C♯	D
A major 3 sharps	A	B	C♯	D	E	F♯	G♯	A
E major 4 sharps	E	F♯	G♯	A	B	C♯	D♯	E
B major 5 sharps	B	C♯	D♯	E	F♯	G♯	A♯	B
F♯ major 6 sharps	F♯	G♯	A♯	B	C♯	D♯	E♯	F♯
C♯ major 7 sharps	C♯	D♯	E♯	F♯	G♯	A♯	B♯	C♯
F major 1 flat	F	G	A	B♭	C	D	E	F
B♭ major 2 flats	B♭	C	D	E♭	F	G	A	B♭
E♭ major 3 flats	E♭	F	G	A♭	B♭	C	D	E♭
A♭ major 4 flats	A♭	B♭	C	D♭	E♭	F	G	A♭
D♭ major 5 flats	D♭	E♭	F	G♭	A♭	B♭	C	D♭
G♭ major 6 flats	G♭	A♭	B♭	C♭	D♭	E♭	F	G♭
C♭ major 7 flats	C♭	D♭	E♭	F♭	G♭	A♭	B♭	C♭

THE TREMOLO

The character of the mandolin is the tremelo. This is accomplished by striking the strings using a down and up motion of the right hand wrist in rapid succession, producing a continuous sound. It could best be described as a series of sixteenth notes played in succession. It is much better not to use a definate rule as to the number of strokes to be made in each beat. Smoothness is the most important factor and requires very much practice.

16th Notes

The tremolo is often written with two short beams across the stem to represent sixteenth notes.

Tremolo is shown in this book with Dotted quarter notes - $1\frac{1}{2}$ counts;

Half notes - 2 counts;

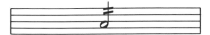

Dotted half notes - 3 counts;

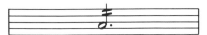

Whole notes - 4 counts;

Notes tied over for one or more counts only show one tremolo sign. The tremolo should last for the complete duration.

5 counts :	6 counts :	7 counts :	8 counts :
	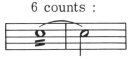	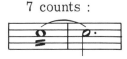	

DOUBLE NOTE EXERCISE USING 6 TH'S
(Across the Fingerboard)

Using All Strings

(Up and Down the Fingerboard)
3rd And 4th String Exercise

2nd And 3rd String Exercise

1st And 2nd String Exercise

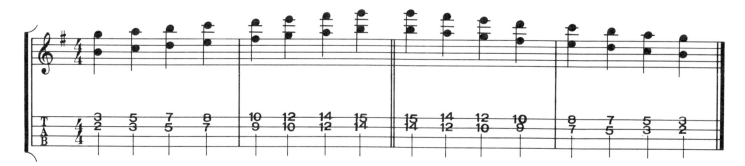

PLAYING 6TH'S ACROSS THE FINGERBOARD

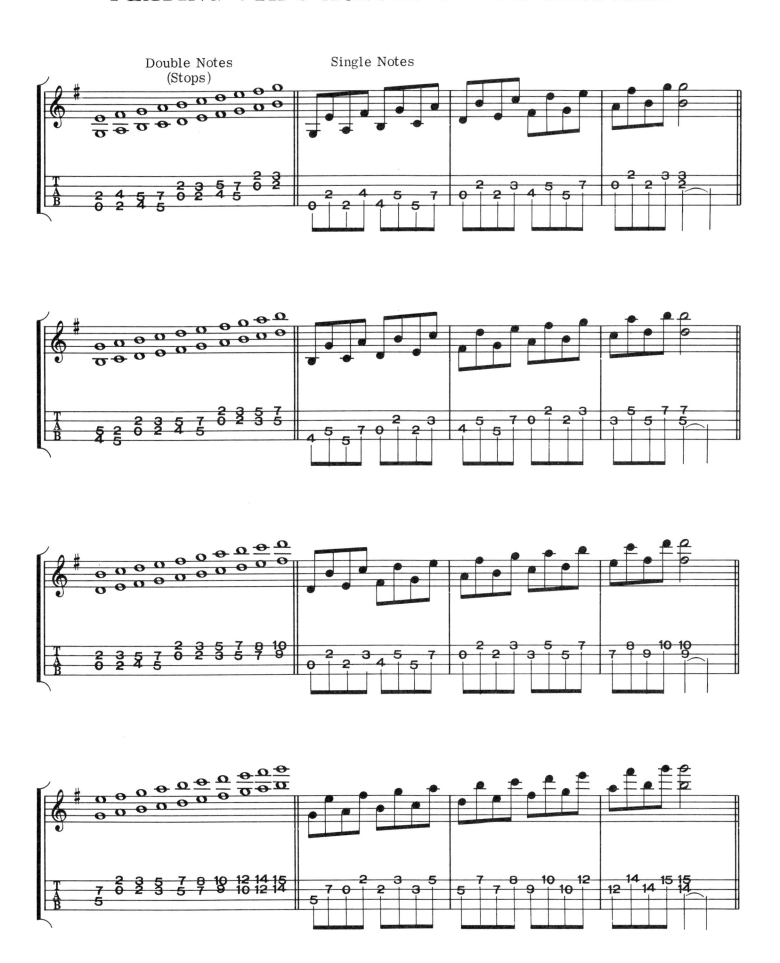

G SCALE EXERCISE USING EIGHTH NOTES

Transpose all exercises to different keys using the major scales starting on page 18.

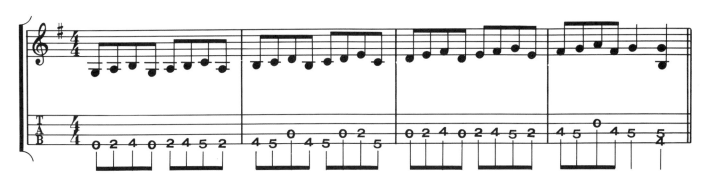

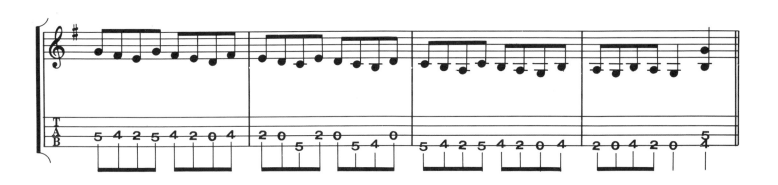

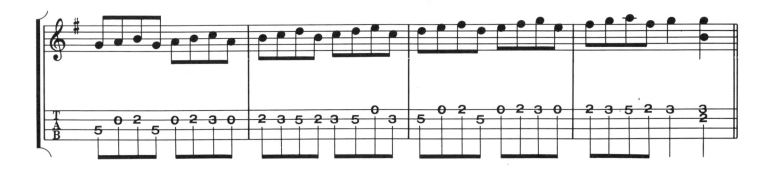

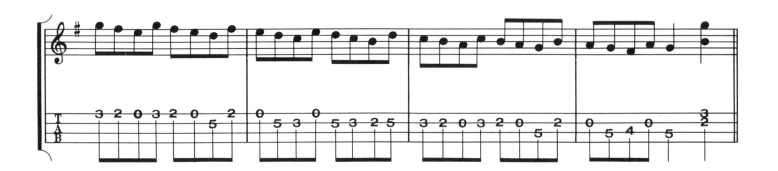

G SCALE EXERCISE USING TRIPLETS

The triplet beat consists of three equal sounds per beat.

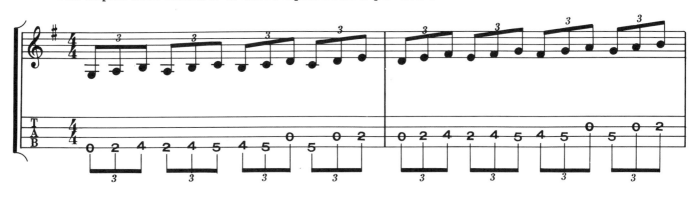

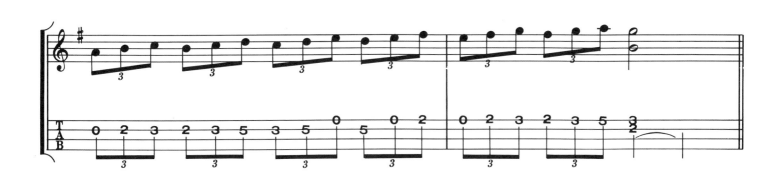

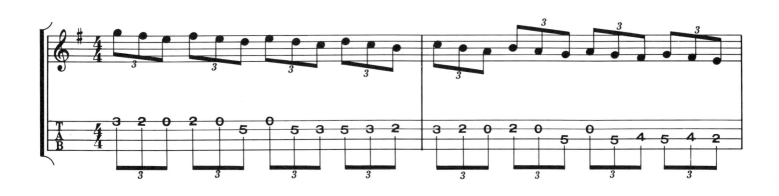

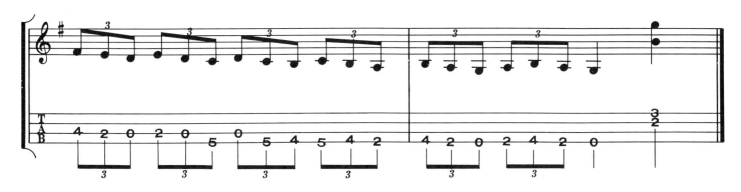

G SCALE EXERCISE IN 6TH S

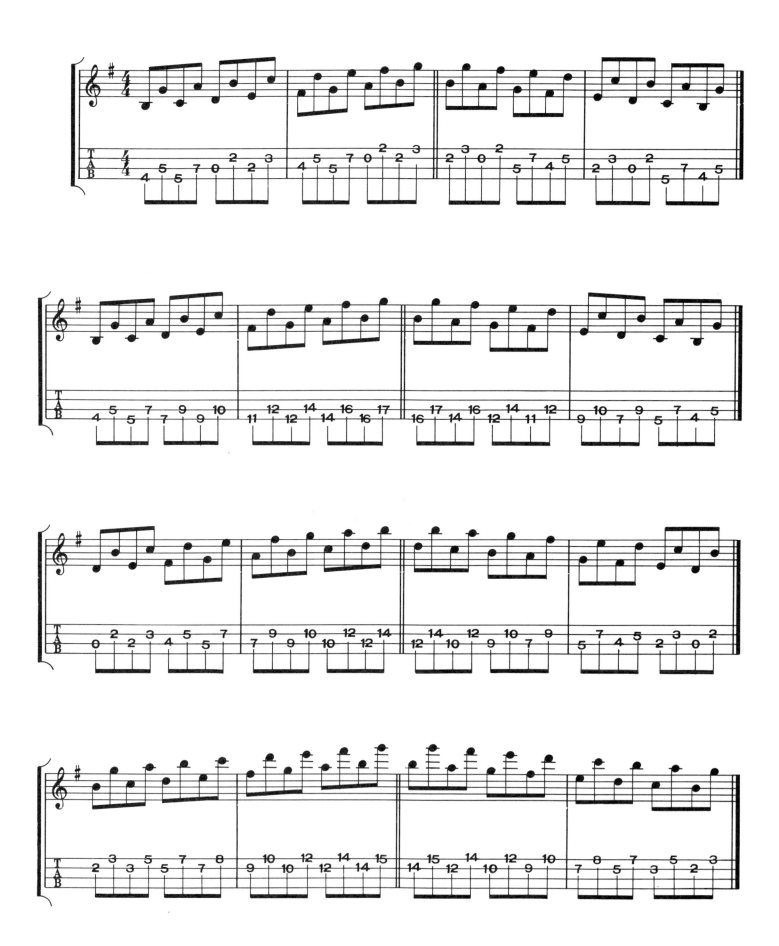

CLASSICAL AND INTERNATIONAL MUSIC SECTION

BOUREE IN E MINOR

Classical
Johann Sebastian Bach

JESU, JOY OF MAN'S DESIRING

Classical Bach

MINUET IN G
(In 3/4 Time)

Classical
Bach
Arranged by
Bud Orr

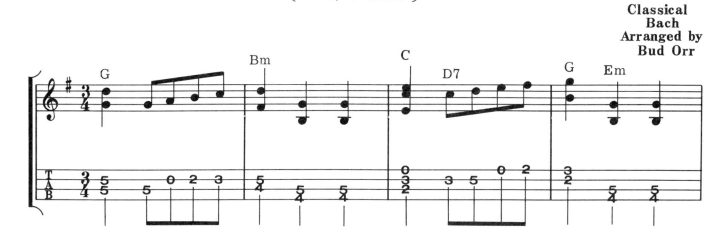

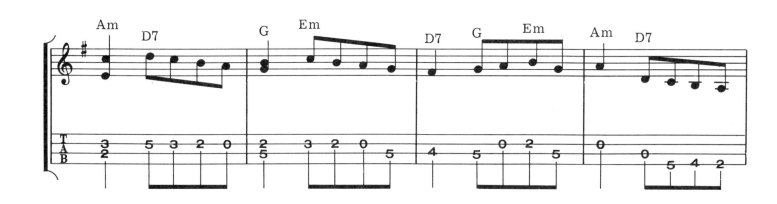

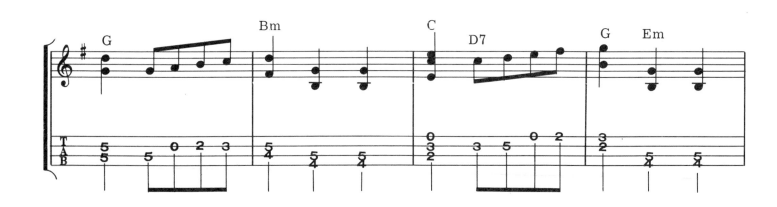

MINUET IN G
(In 4/4 Time)

Classical
Bach
Arranged by
Bud Orr

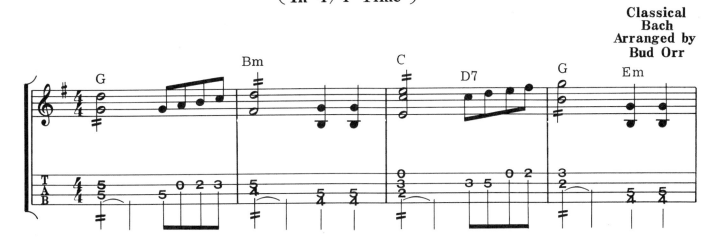

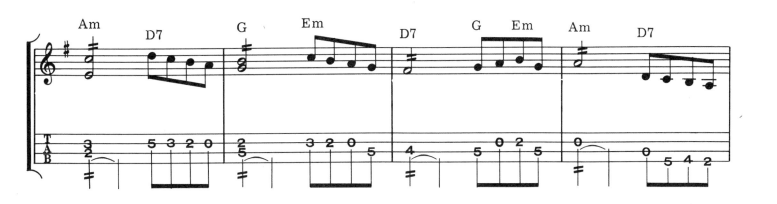

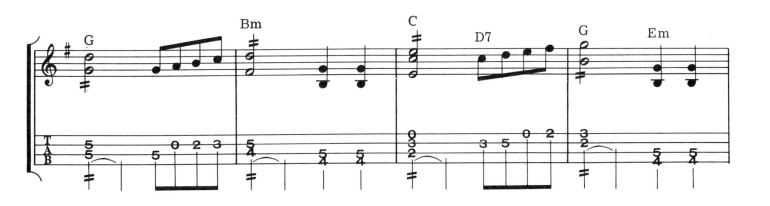

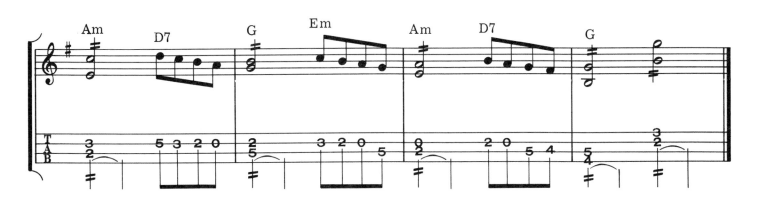

LIEBESTRAUM

Classical
Franz Liszt

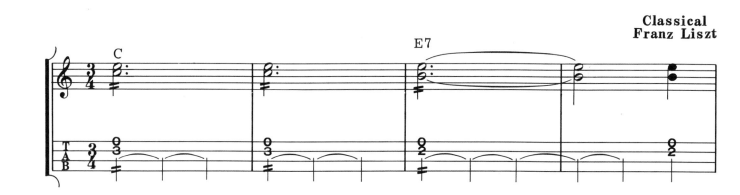

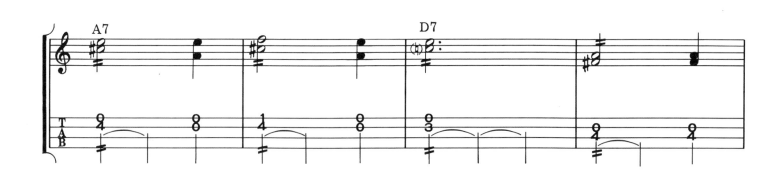

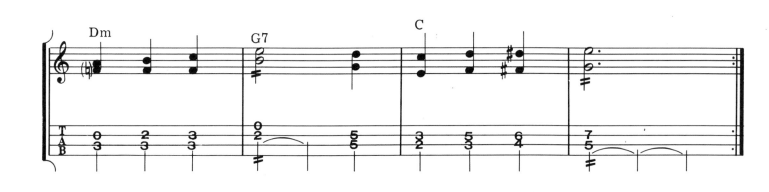

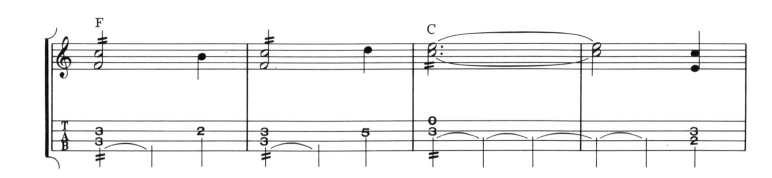

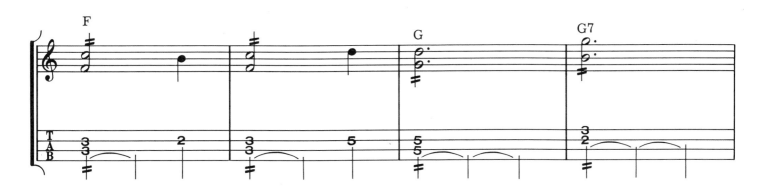

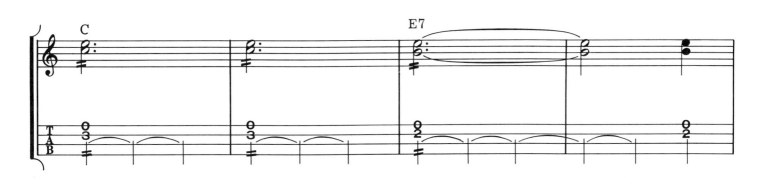

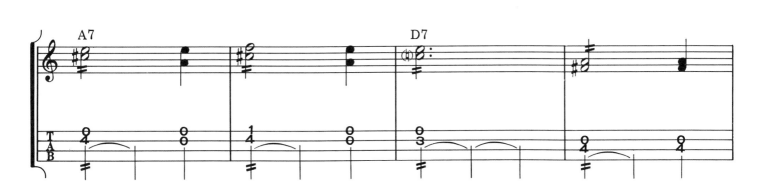

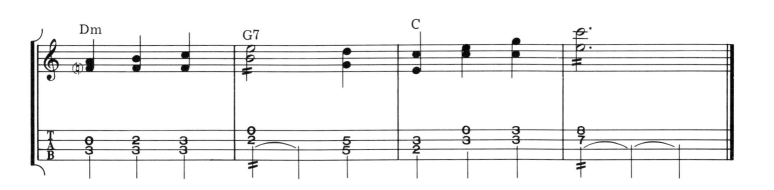

BEETHOVEN'S 9TH SYMPHONY
(Ode to Joy)

Classical
L. Van Beethoven

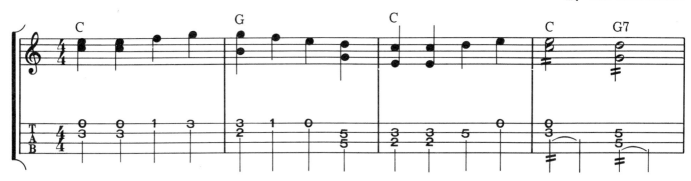

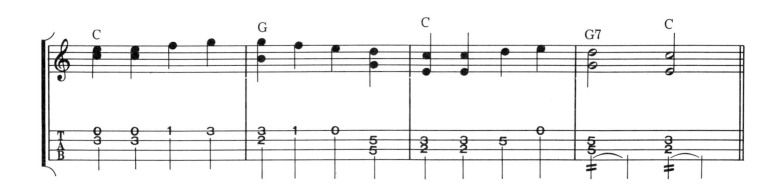

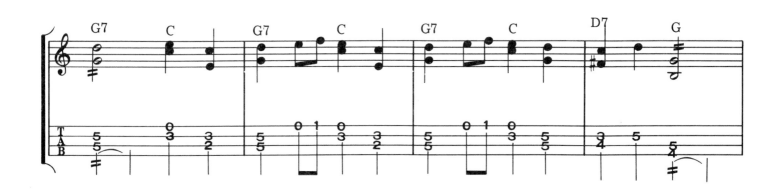

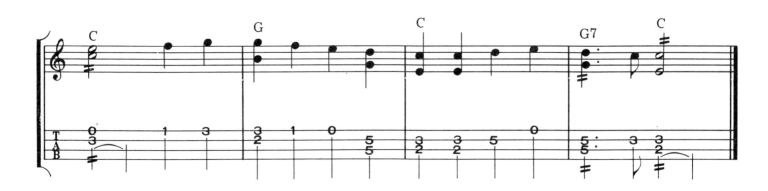

CIRIBIRIBIN

Italian

39

O SOLE MIO

Italian

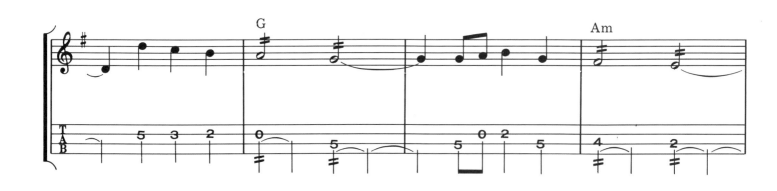

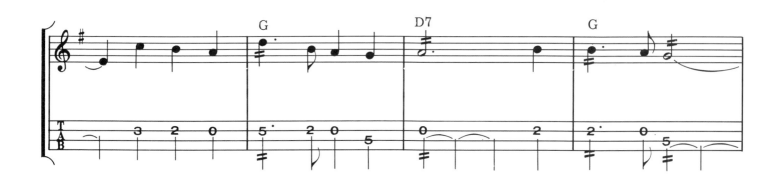

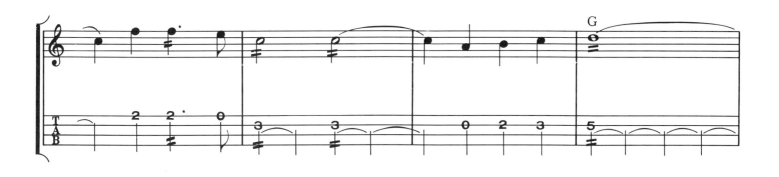

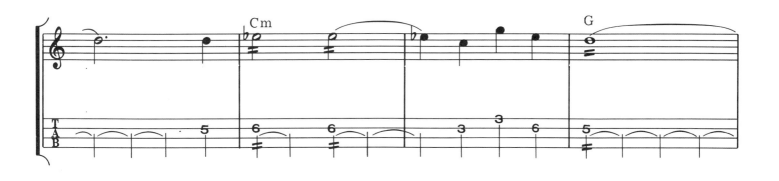

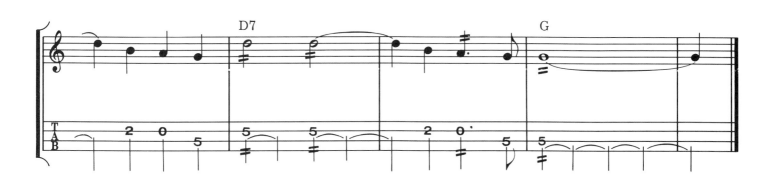

CARNIVAL OF VENICE

Italian

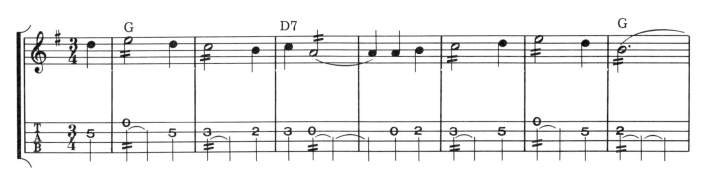

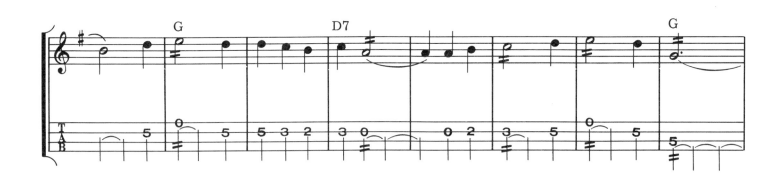

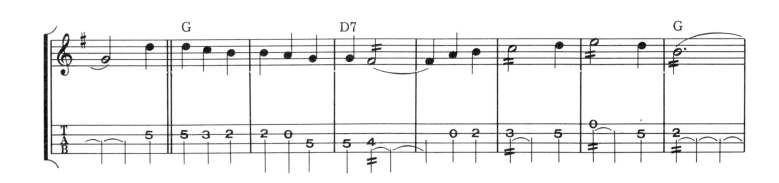

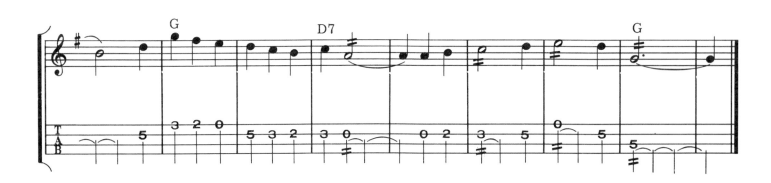

SANTA LUCIA

Italian

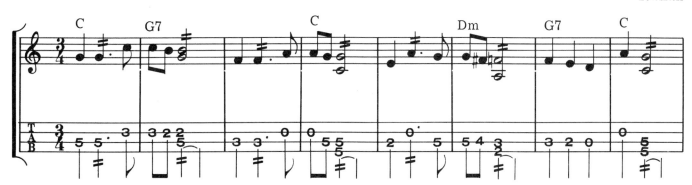

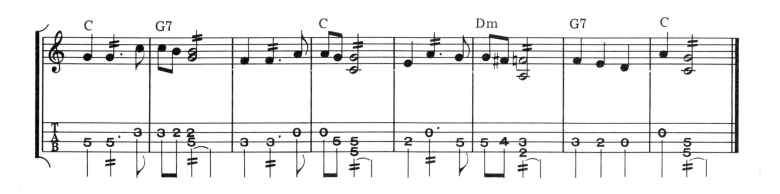

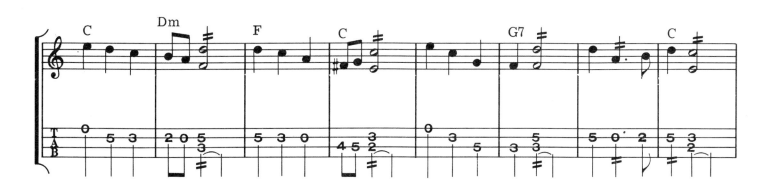

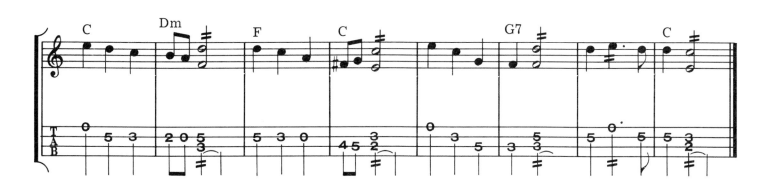

SORRENTO

Italian

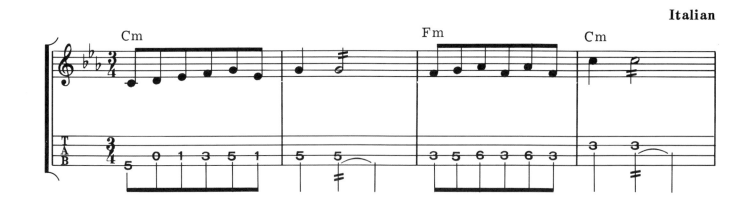

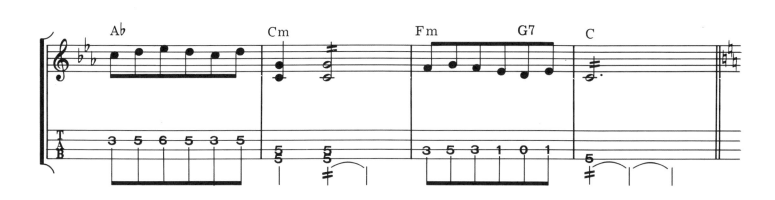

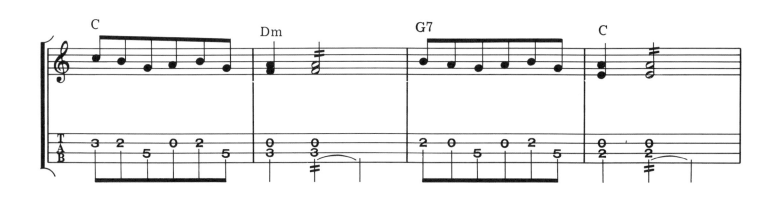

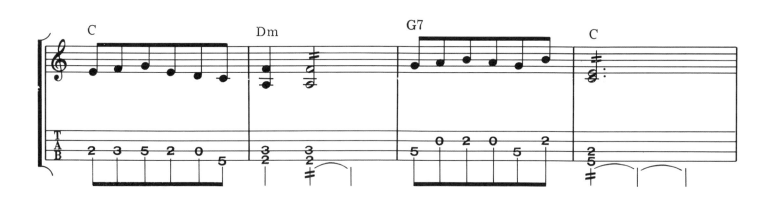

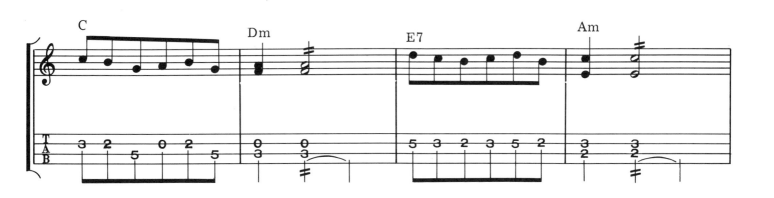

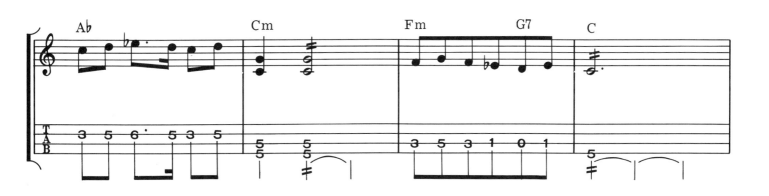

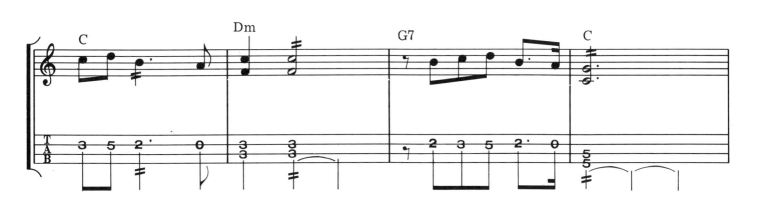

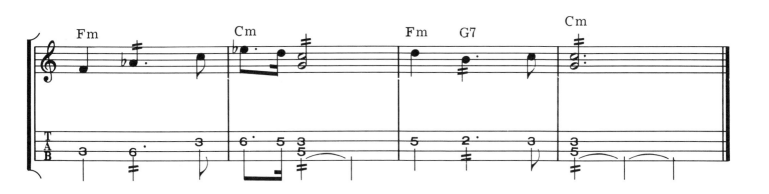

OH, MARIE

Italian

LA SPAGNOLA

Spanish

LA GOLONDRINA

Spanish

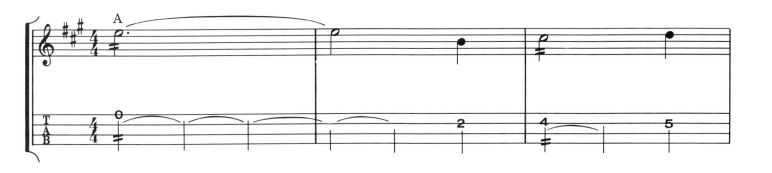

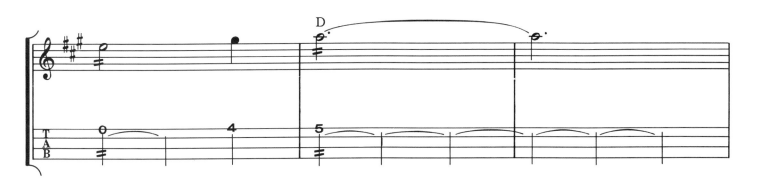

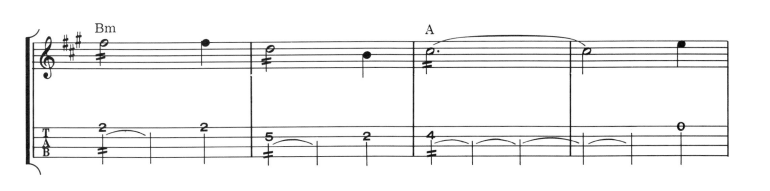

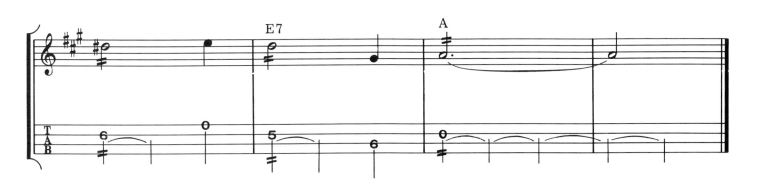

LA PALOMA
(The Dove)

Mexican

VIVA L'AMOR

French

ALOUETTE

French

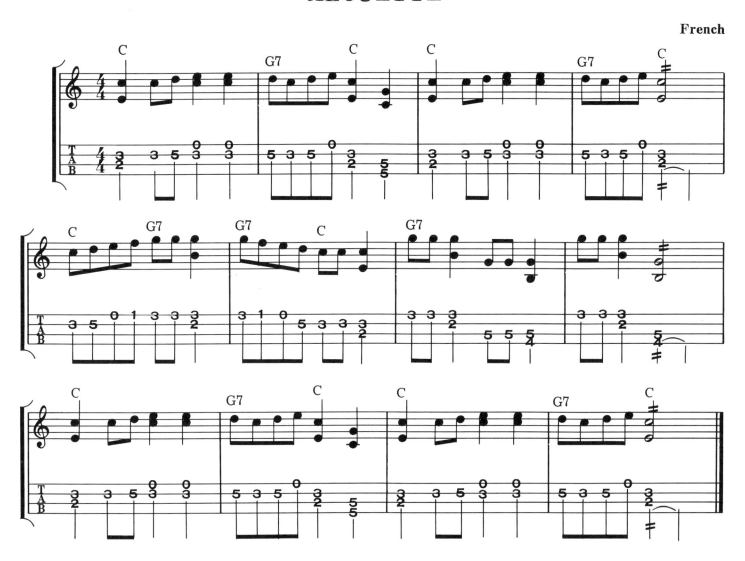

THE FRENCH SONG

French

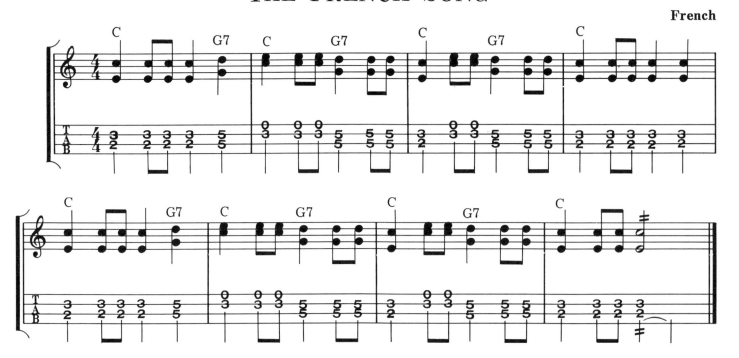

TWO GUITARS

Russian

DARK EYES

Russian

MOSCOW NIGHTS

Russian

DANUBE WAVES

German

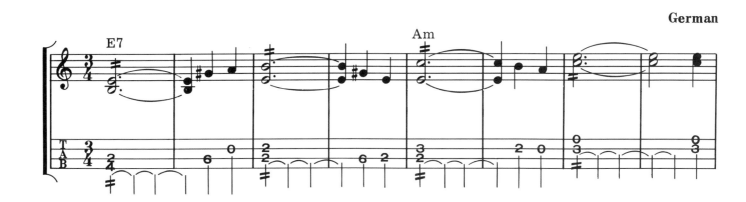

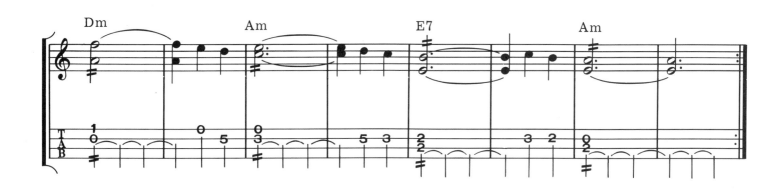

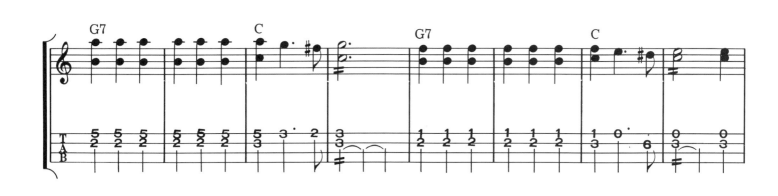

GERMAN FOLK SONG

German

HAVA NAGILA

Israeli Hora

MINKA, MINKA

Yiddish
Folk Song

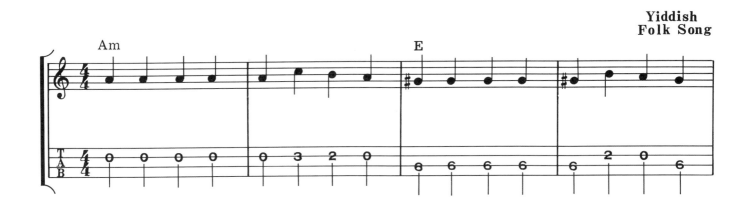

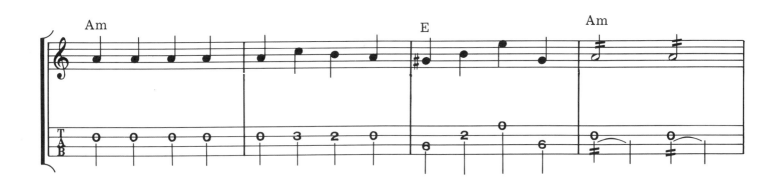

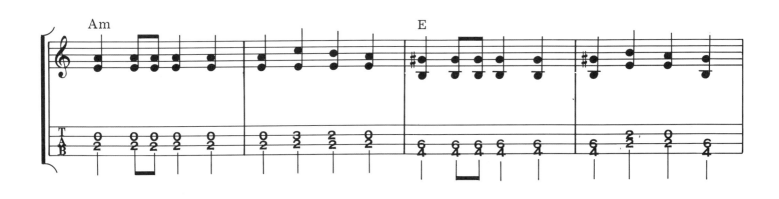

CIELITO LINDO

Mexican

HI-LI , HI-LO

French

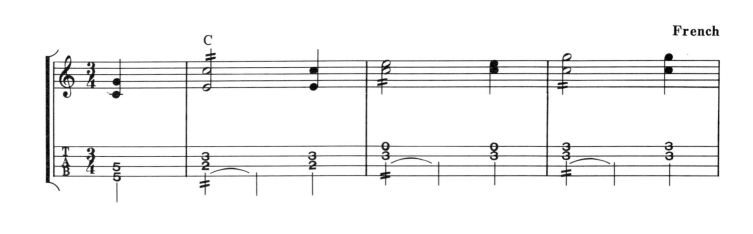

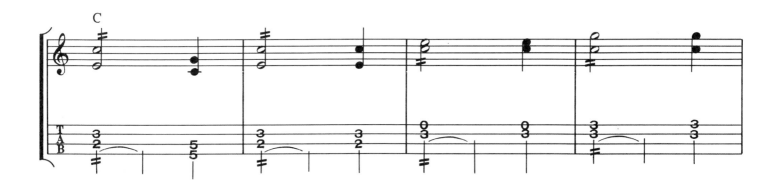

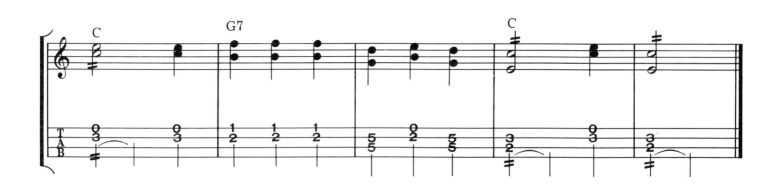

PLAY, BOUZOUKI, PLAY
(A Tribute to the Greek Bouzouki)

Bud Orr

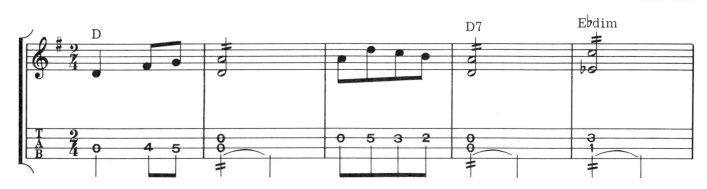

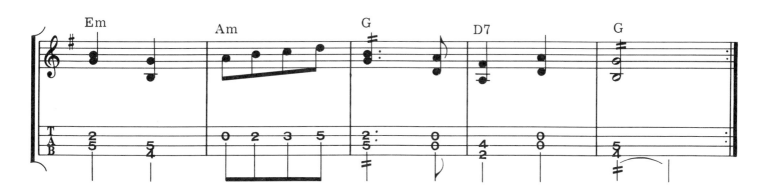

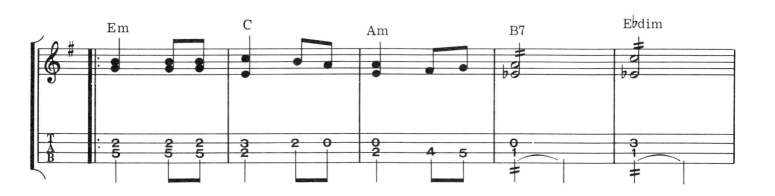

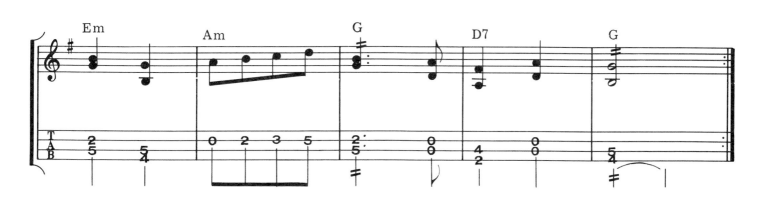

PLAY , FIDDLE , PLAY

Gypsy

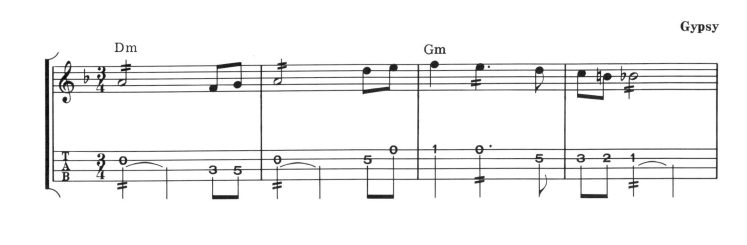

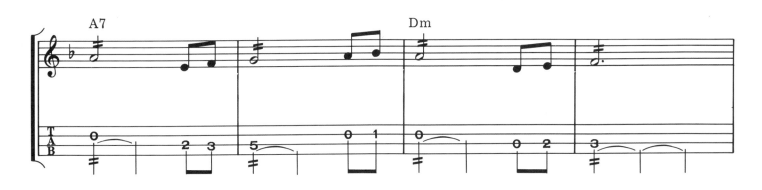

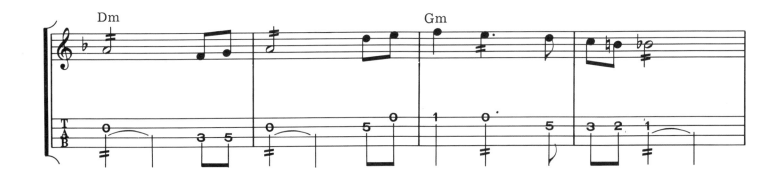

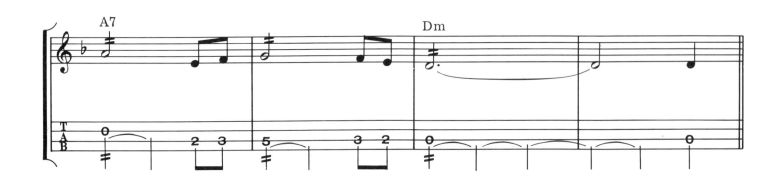

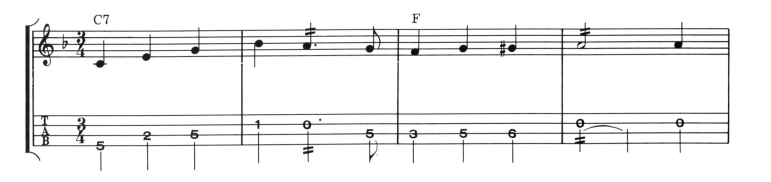

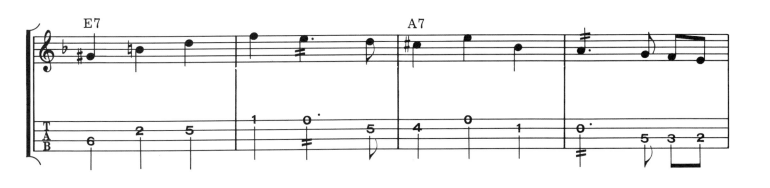

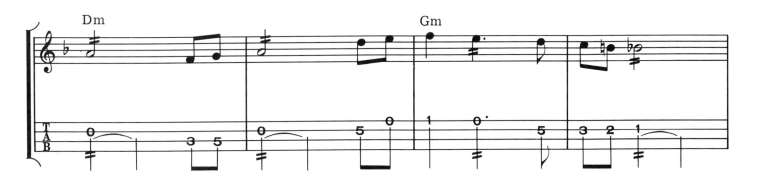

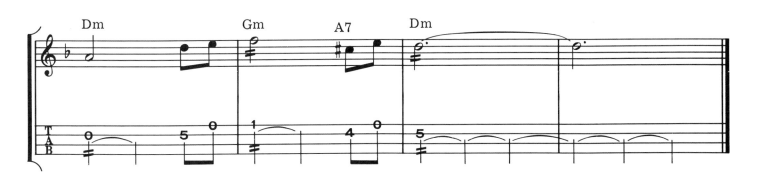

LONDONDERRY AIR

Irish

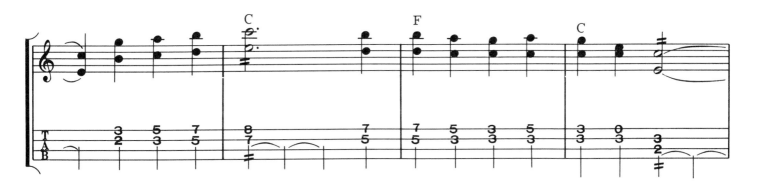

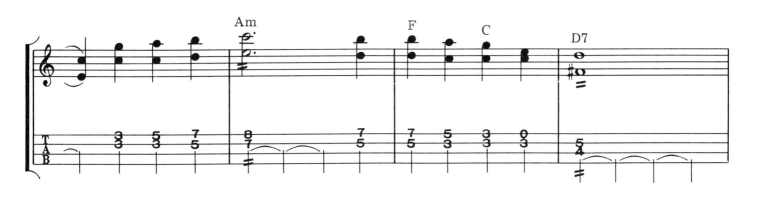

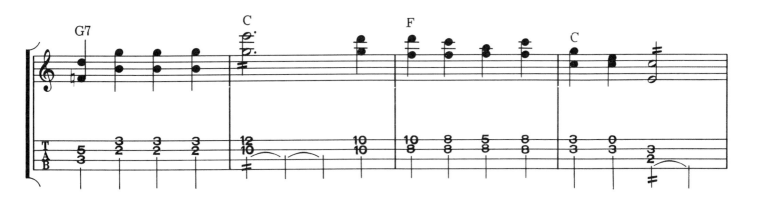

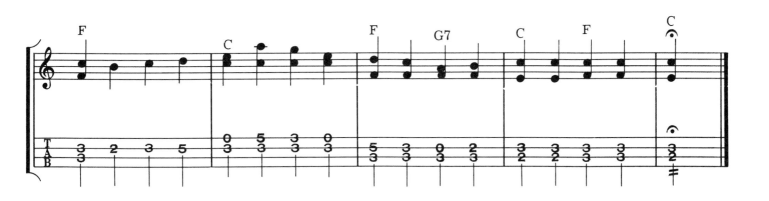

GREENSLEEVES
(In 3/4 Time)

Old English

GREENSLEEVES
(In 4/4 Time)

Old English

I GAVE MY LOVE A CHERRY

English Folk

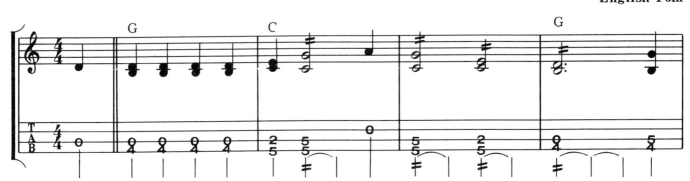

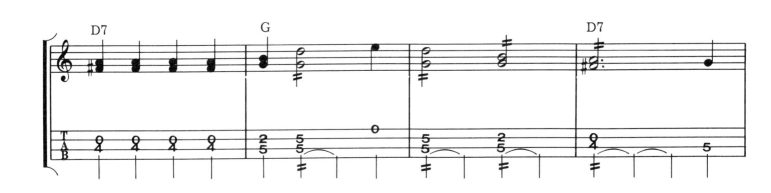

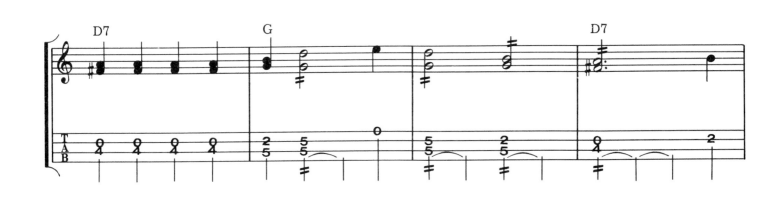

SCARLET RIBBONS

Traditional

COCKLES AND MUSSELS

Irish

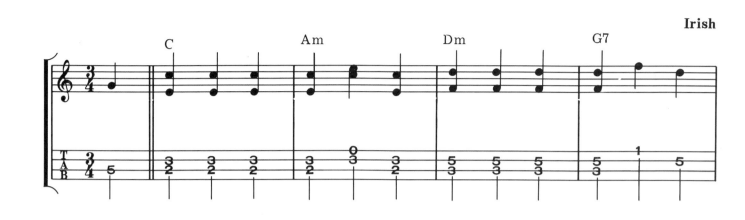

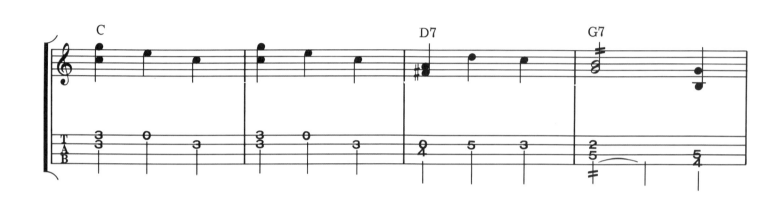

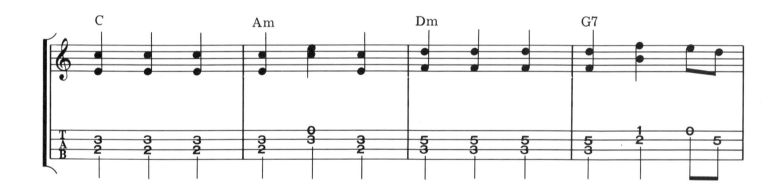

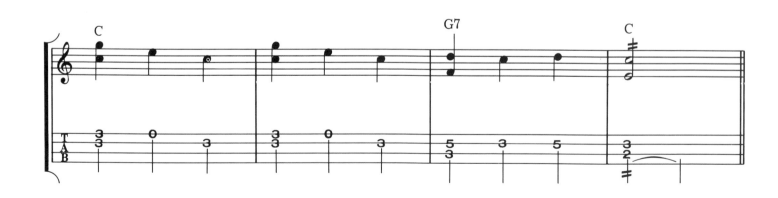

LOCH LOMOND

Scottish

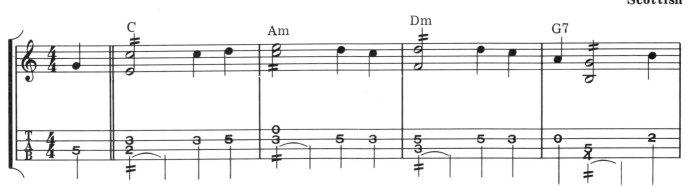

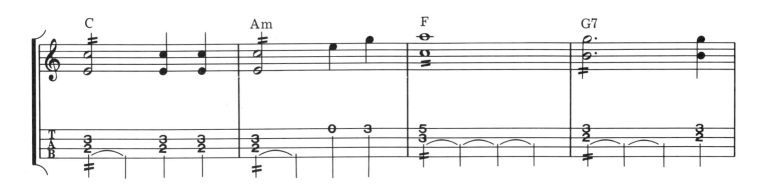

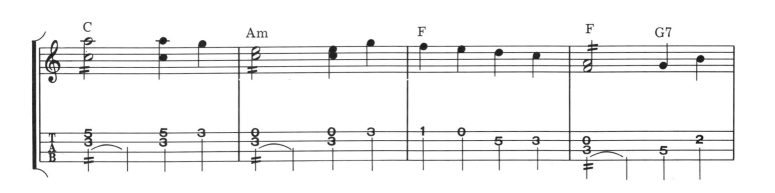

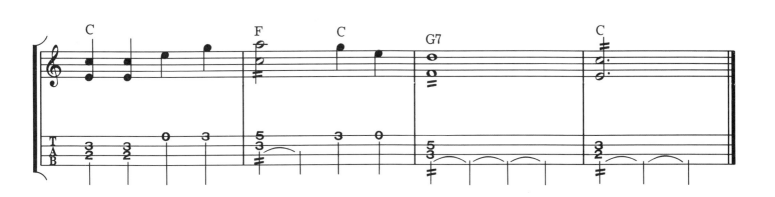

SCARBOROUGH FAIR

Traditional

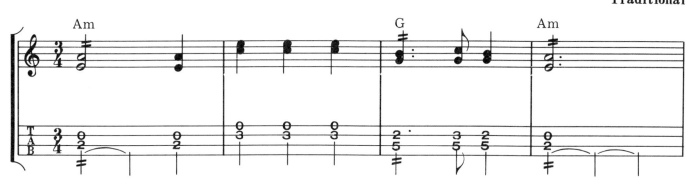

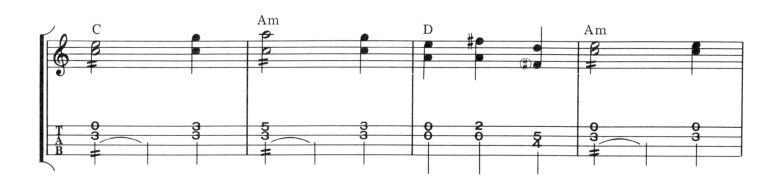

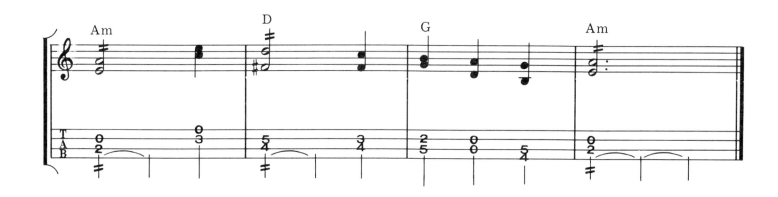

WAYFARING STRANGER

Traditional

OVER THE WAVES

Traditional

BLUE MIDNIGHT WALTZ

Bud Orr

AURA LEE

Traditional

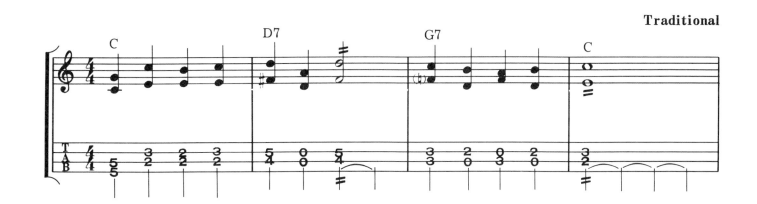

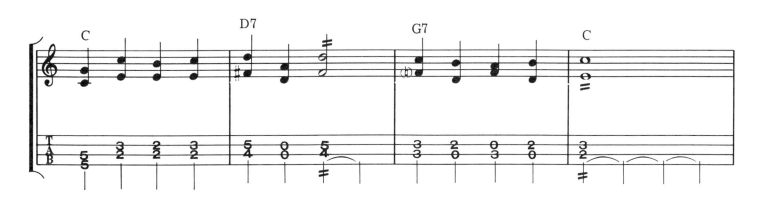

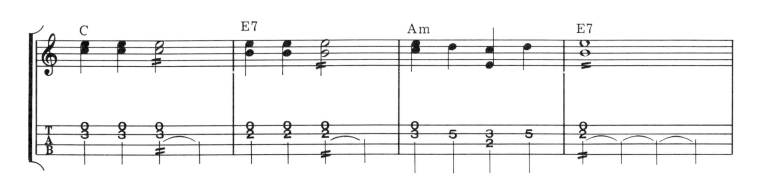

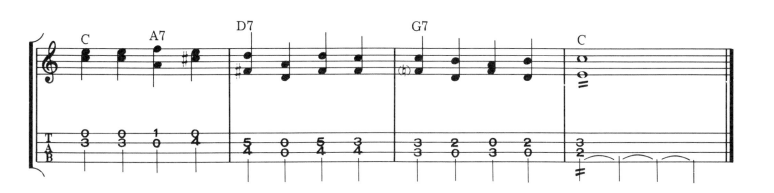

FANTASY WALTZ

Bud Orr

LOOK DOWN THAT LONESOME ROAD

Traditional

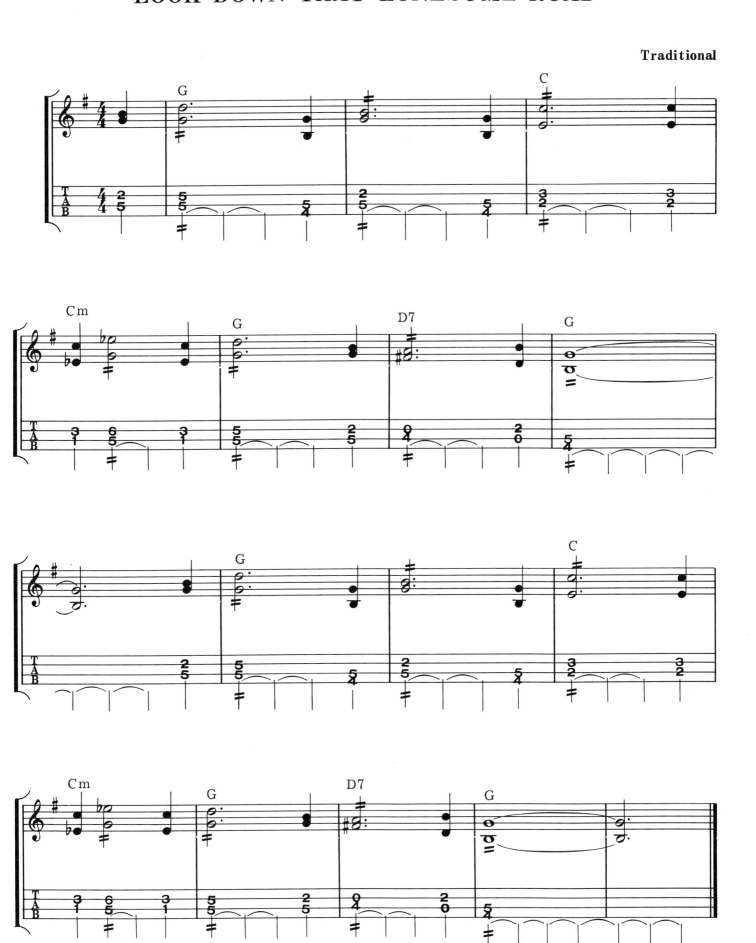

THE RISING SUN

Traditional

STREETS OF LAREDO

American Western

83

HOME ON THE RANGE

American Western

SHENANDOAH

Folk

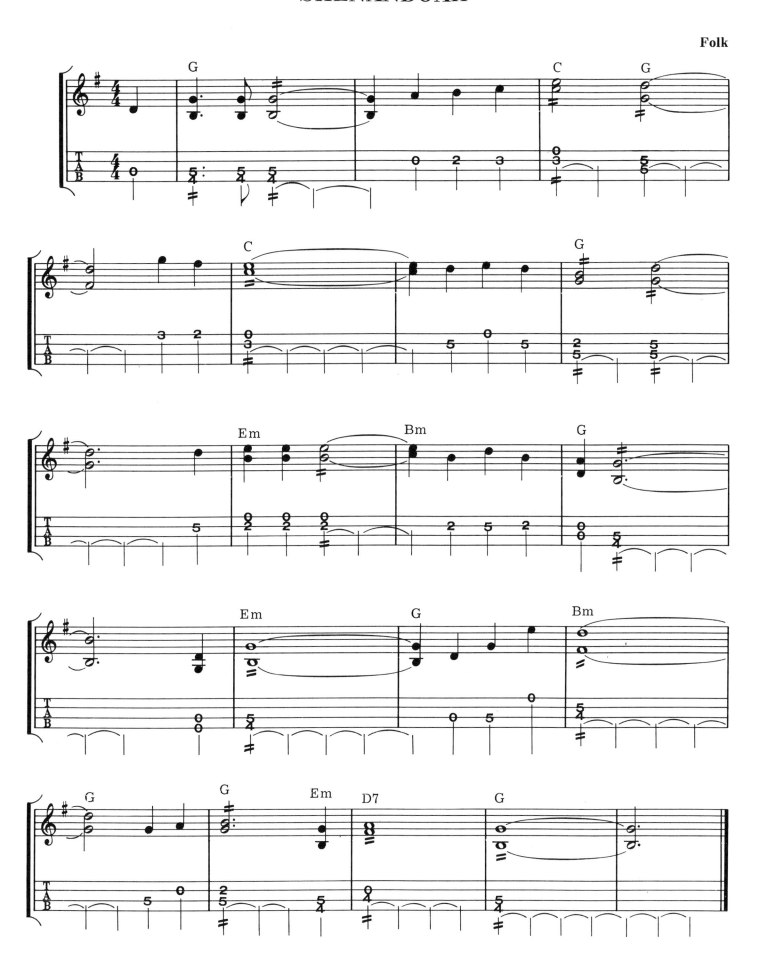

BEAUTIFUL DREAMER

Stephen Foster

FRANKIE AND JOHNNY

Traditional
Folk

CHORD AND RHYTHM BACKGROUND SECTION

This section includes the following:

CHORD SYMBOLS AND HOW TO USE THEM
EASY MANDOLIN STRUMS
MANDOLIN CHORDS—INCLUDING:
MAJOR CHORDS
MINOR CHORDS
SEVENTH CHORDS
SIXTH CHORDS
MINOR SIXTH CHORDS
MAJOR SEVENTH CHORDS
MINOR SEVENTH CHORDS
NINTH CHORDS
AUGMENTED CHORDS
DIMINISHED CHORDS
MOVABLE CHORDS

THE CHORD SYMBOL

A chord symbol is a drawing of the mandolin neck. Hold the mandolin in front of you so that you are facing the fingerboard. (The 1st string should be on your right.)

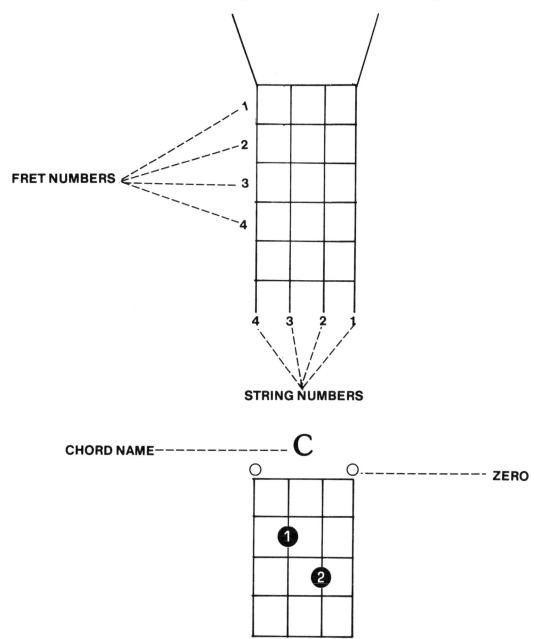

The numbers on the fret diagrams show where to place the left hand fingers.

A zero (0) indicates that the string marked is to be played open.

An (X) indicates that the string is not to be played. When 2 or 3 fingers of the left hand are used to form a chord it is very important to put them all down at the same time so that a change from one chord position to another can be made quickly and smoothly.

Easy Mandolin Strums

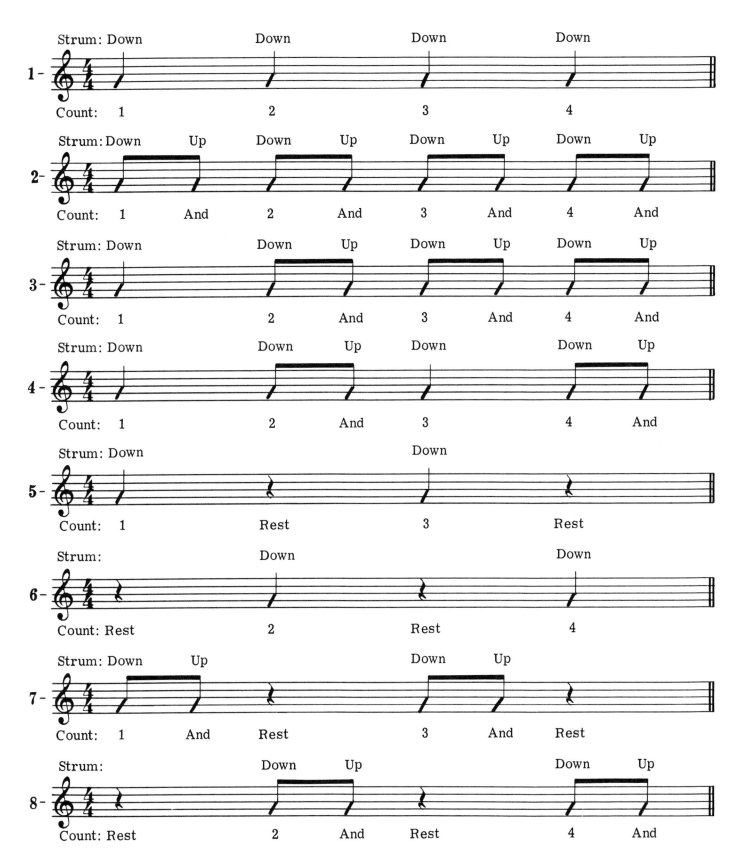

See Mel Bay's "Fun With Strums" Book For Further Study.

MANDOLIN CHORDS

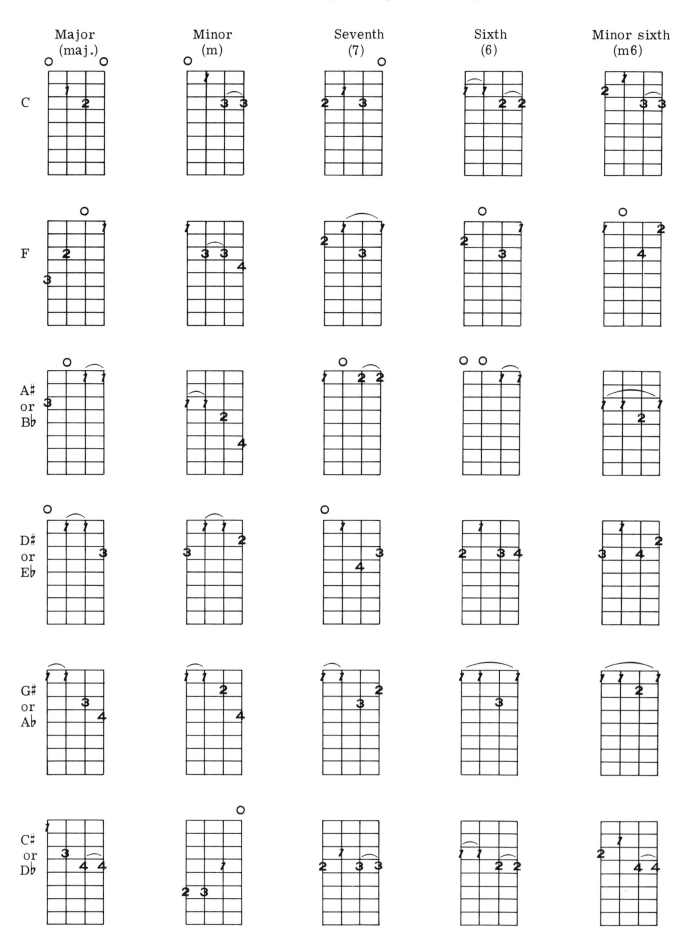

MANDOLIN CHORDS

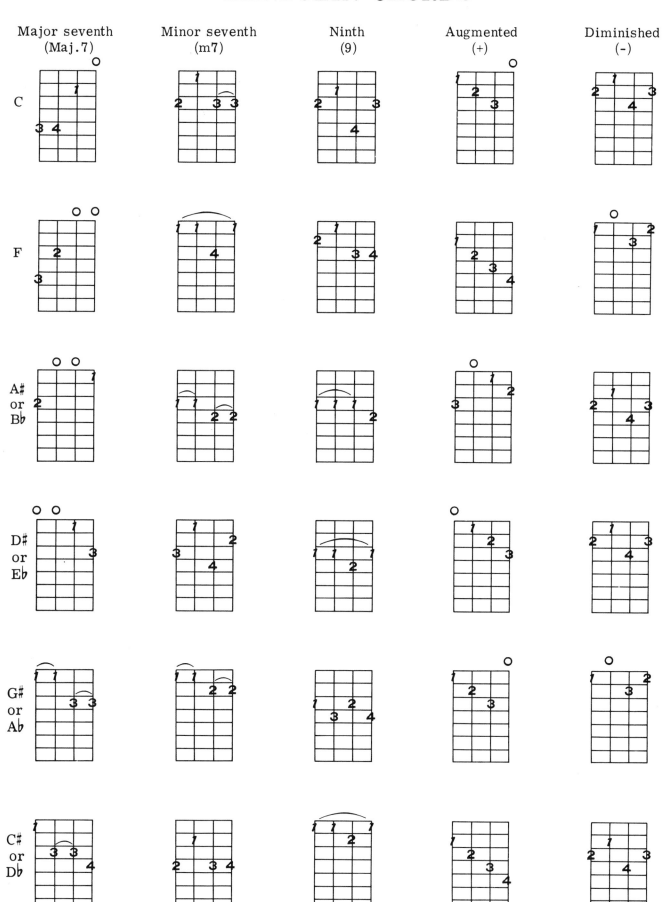

MANDOLIN CHORDS

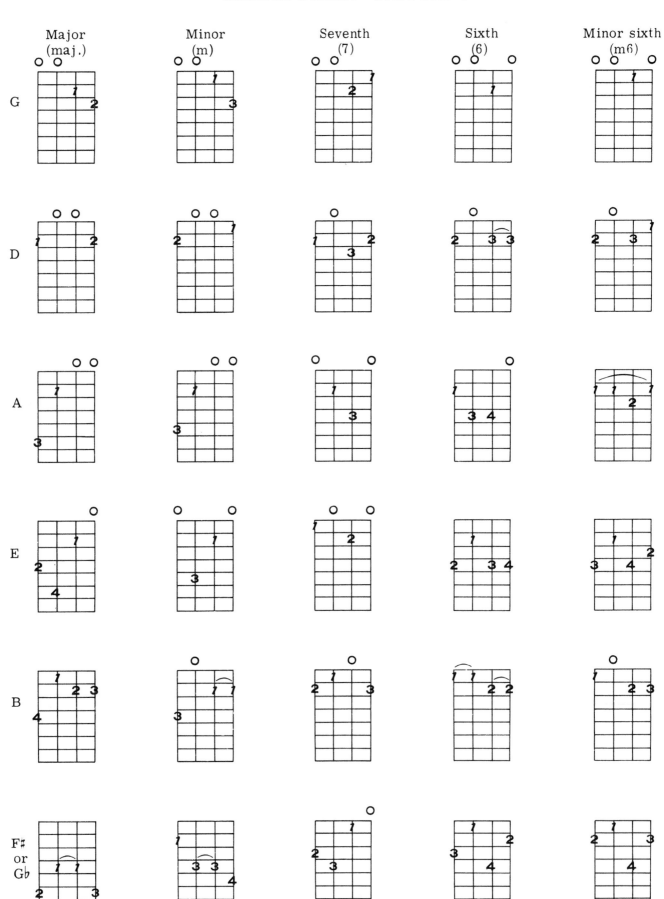

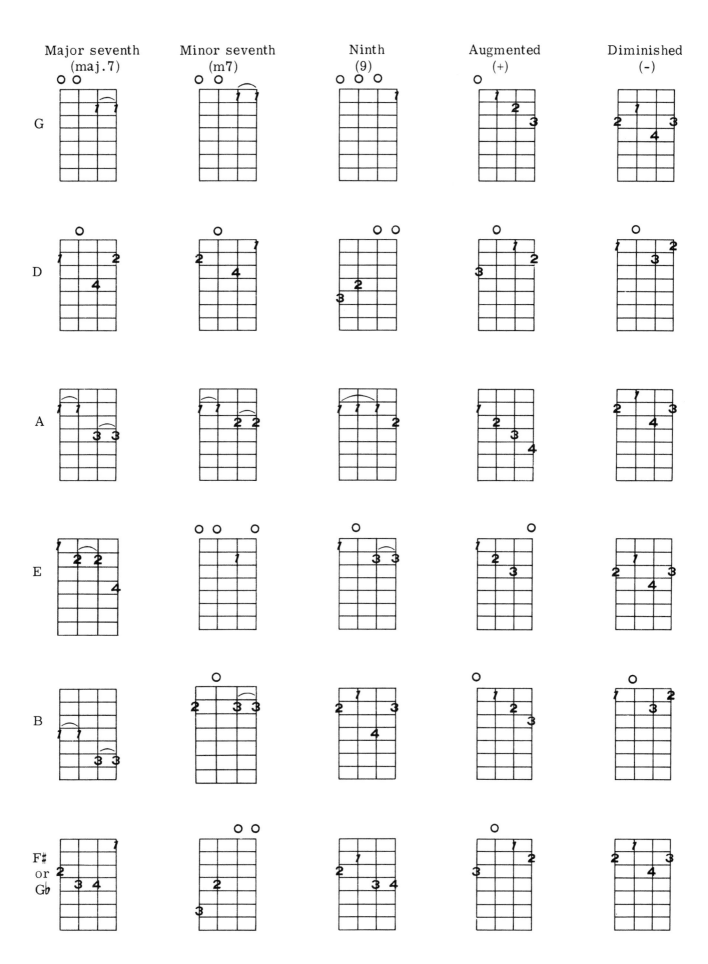

Movable Chords

A movable chord consists of three or more fingered strings played together with no open strings. The chart below contains all fingered strings. This means that you can shift your hand position up or down the fingerboard and for each fret, the chord will have a different name. All chords shown are in the second position. This means that you can shift down one fret, or up the fingerboard as far as you can physically reach, and still get a good sound.

D
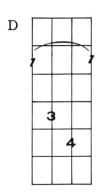

E
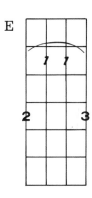

G
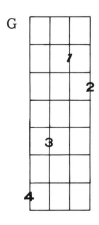

A
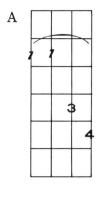

A7
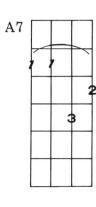

Fret	Chord
1	C# or Db
2	D
3	D# or Eb
4	E
5	F
6	F# or Gb

Fret	Chord
1	D# or Eb
2	E
3	F
4	F# or Gb
5	G
6	G# or Ab

Fret	Chord
1	F# or Gb
2	G
3	G# or Ab
4	A
5	A# or Bb
6	B

Fret	Chord
1	G# or Ab
2	A
3	A# or Bb
4	B
5	C
6	C# or Db

Fret	Chord
1	G#7 or Ab7
2	A7
3	A#7 or Bb7
4	B7
5	C7
6	C#7 or Db7

C7
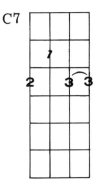

E7
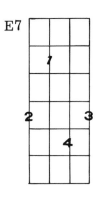

Am
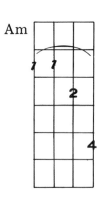

Dm
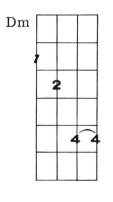

A#dim.

Fret	Chord
1	B7
2	C7
3	C#7 or Db7
4	D7
5	D#7 or Eb7
6	E7

Fret	Chord
1	D#7 or Eb7
2	E7
3	F7
4	F#7 or Gb7
5	G7
6	G#7 or Ab7

Fret	Chord
1	G#m or Abm
2	Am
3	A#m or Bbm
4	Bm
5	Cm
6	C#m or Dbm

Fret	Chord
1	C#m or Dbm
2	Dm
3	D#m or Ebm
4	Em
5	Fm
6	F#m or Gbm

Diminished chords can be named from any note you are holding down. Refer to the fingerboard chart on page 17

PICKING TECHNIQUE SECTION

This section includes the following:

THE BASIC MANDOLIN PICKING EFFECTS
EXERCISES FOR PICKING EFFECTS
FILLS AND ENDINGS IN G
FILLS AND ENDINGS IN C
FILLS AND ENDINGS IN D
FILLS AND ENDINGS IN A

Note:
Fills and endings are shown in the 4 most widely
used keys for country and bluegrass music.
Practice transposing to other keys using
the Major scales starting on page 18.

The Basic Mandolin Picking Effects

The three effects other than tremolo that are used in mandolin playing are shown below. Practice them over and over until each is clear sounding and even. In each example, you pick the string only once but two seperate notes are sounded. Always pick the first note a little harder when sliding, hammering, or pulling off so that both notes will be heard clearly before the sound fades away.

The Slide

Pick the 1st note of each slide in the normal way; then keeping the left hand finger pressed firmly down, slide quickly to the 2nd note which is found in the fret shown in the tablature.

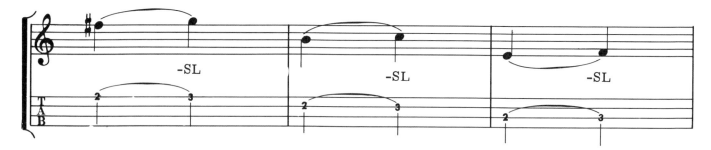

The Hammer

Pick the 1st note of each hammer in the normal way. To obtain the 2nd note.tap the left hand finger down hard and fast on the string.

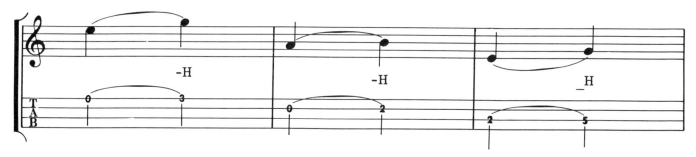

The Pull-Off

Pick the 1st note of each "pull-off" in the normal way. To obtain the 2nd note, use the left hand finger you are pushing the string down with to pluck or push the in a downward direction.

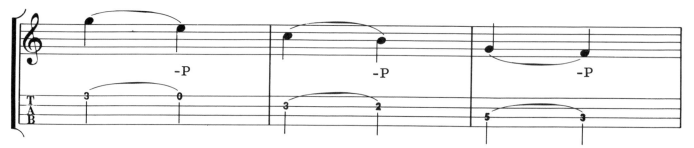

EXERCISES FOR PICKING EFFECTS

SLIDE EXERCISE

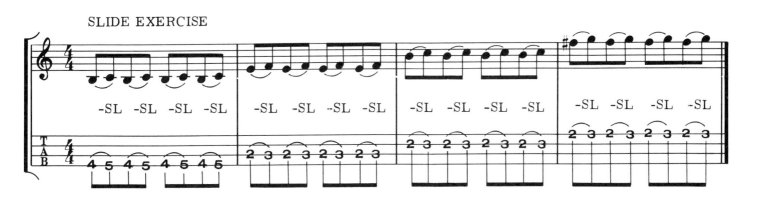

HAMMER EXERCISE

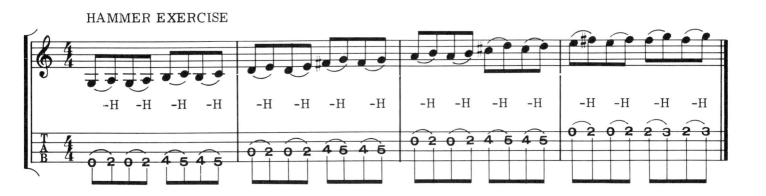

PULL-OFF EXERCISE

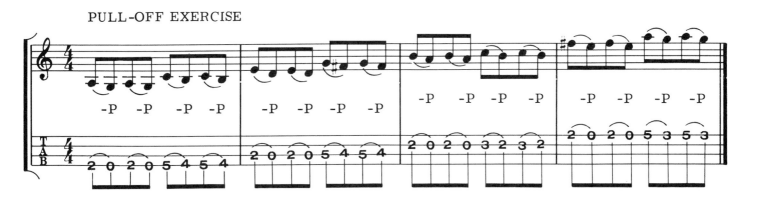

MIXED EFFECTS

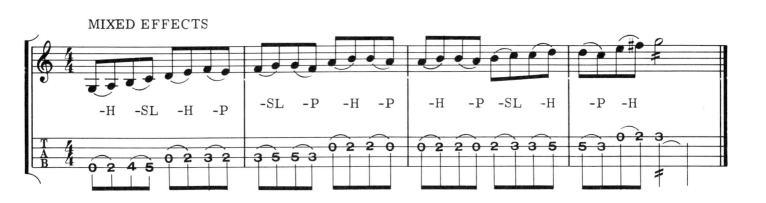

Fills and Endings

When a melody note is held for several counts (4 to 8 counts), fills are used on the mandolin.
Go back and experiment from the very first song. Many are used in these arrangements.

Fills and Endings in G

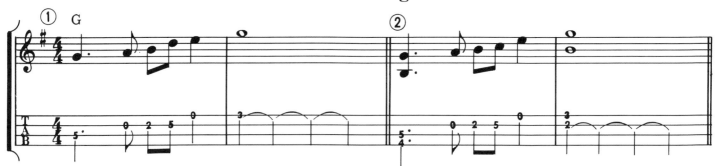

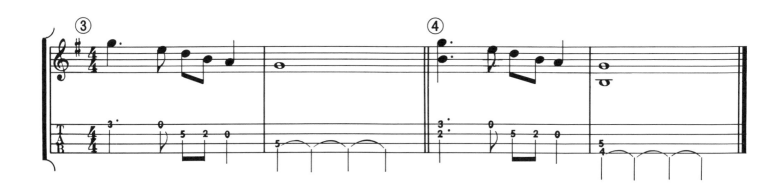

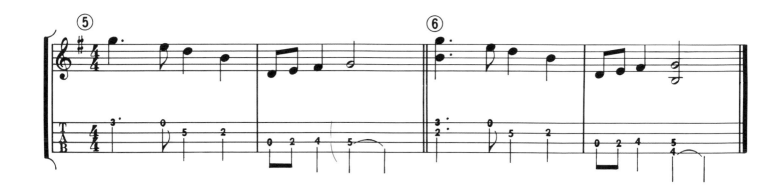

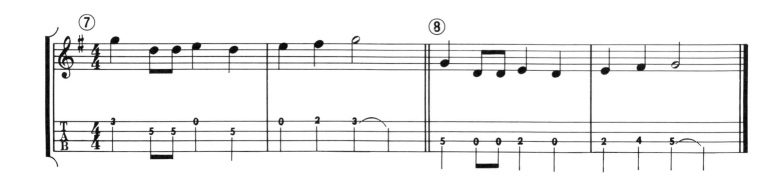

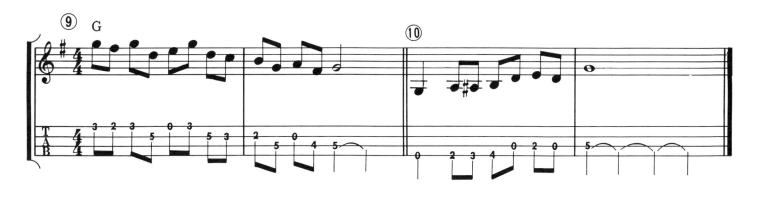

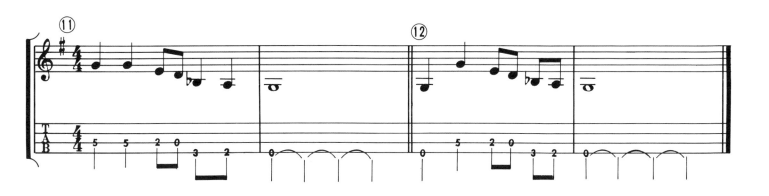

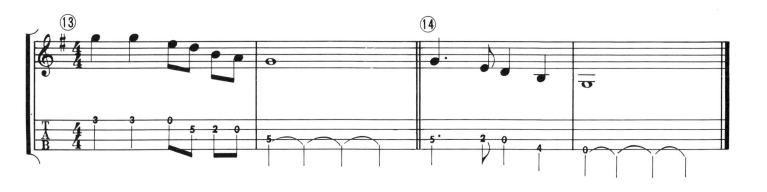

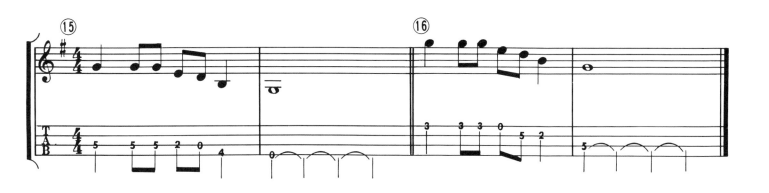

Fills and Endings in C

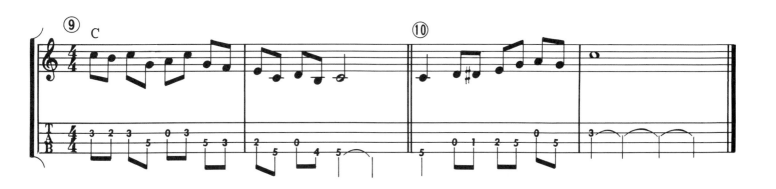

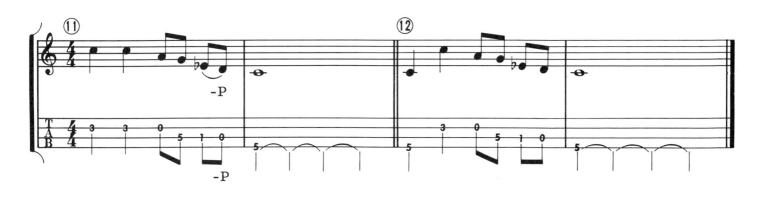

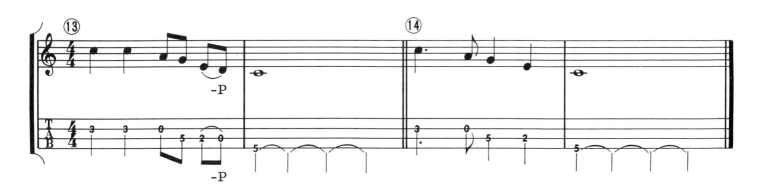

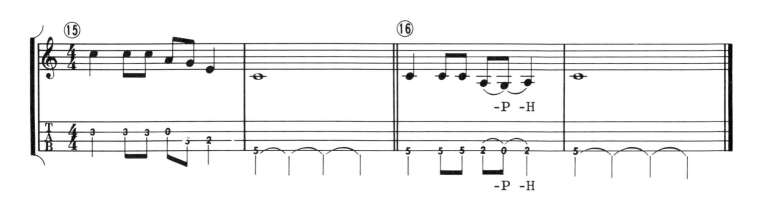

Fills and Endings in D

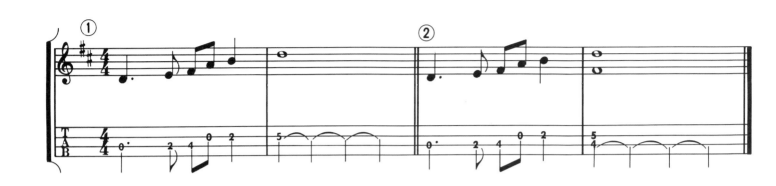

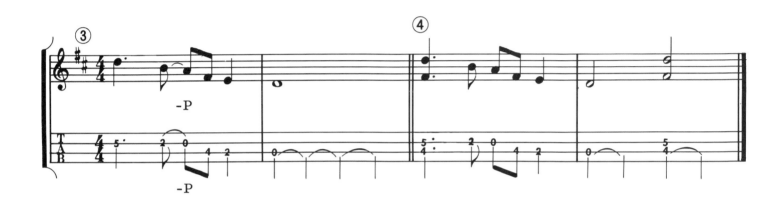

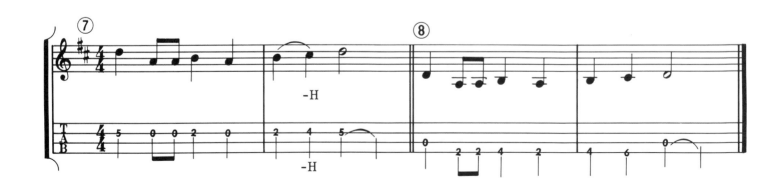

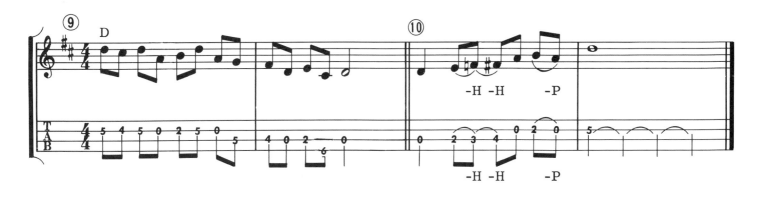

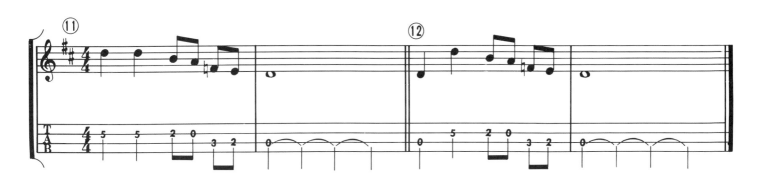

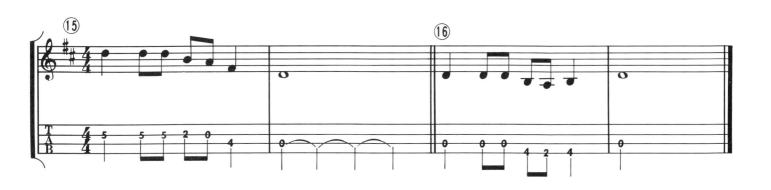

Fills and Endings in A

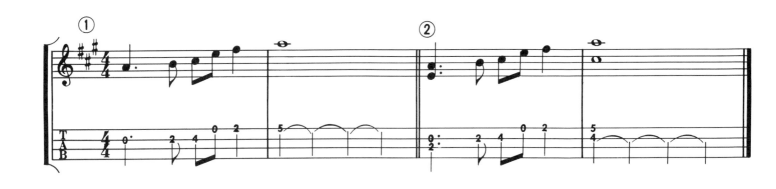

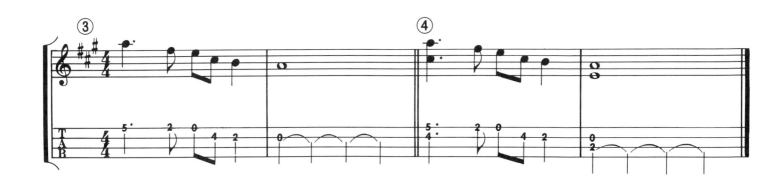

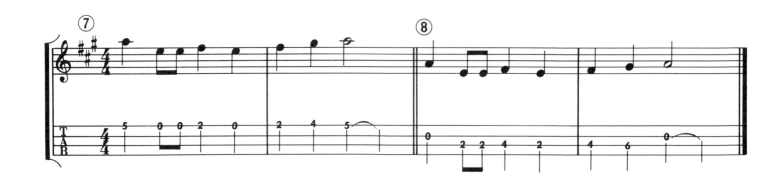

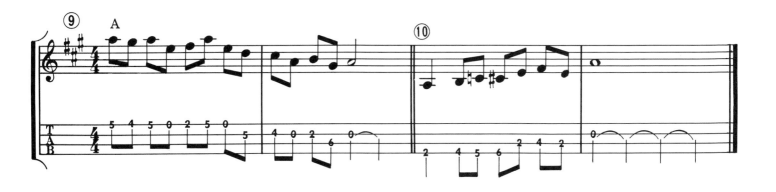

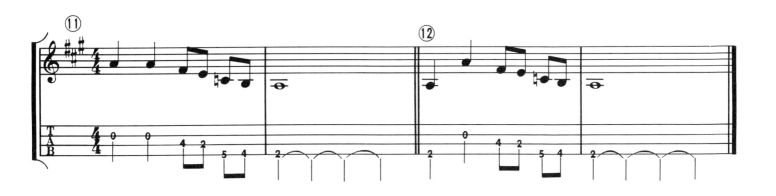

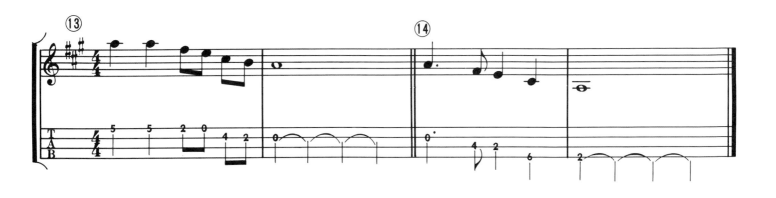

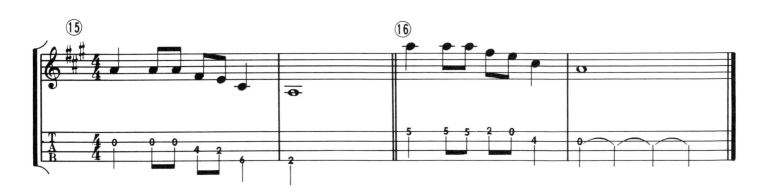

MANDOLIN STYLES

Gourd shaped back

"A" Model

Florentine Model

"F" Model

EARLY COUNTRY AND BLUEGRASS MUSIC SECTION

LITTLE ROSEWOOD CASKET

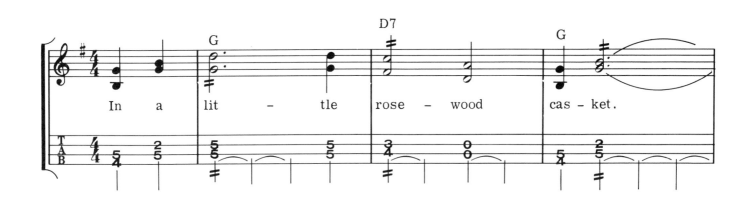

In a lit — tle rose — wood cas — ket.

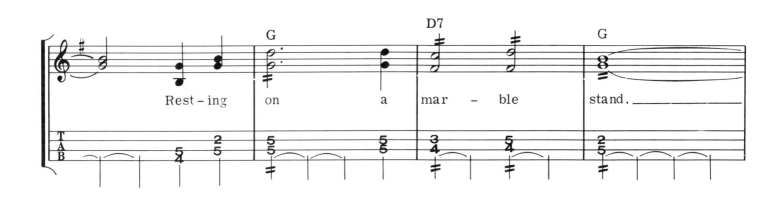

Rest — ing on a mar — ble stand.____

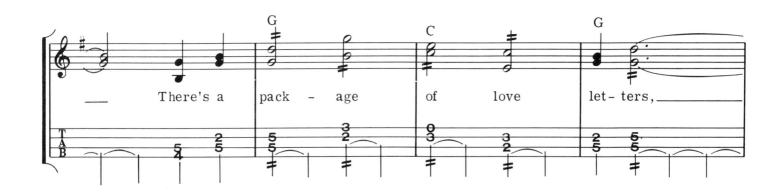

____ There's a pack — age of love let — ters,____

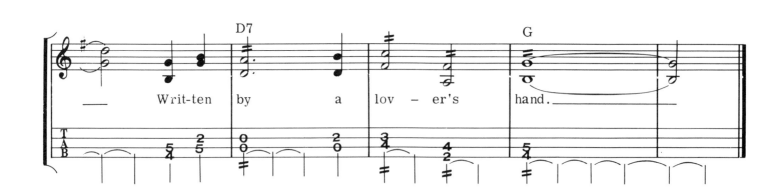

____ Writ — ten by a lov — er's hand.____

I'M JUST HERE TO GET MY BABY OUT OF JAIL

I'm not in your town to stay, said a la-dy old and grey, to the war-den of the pen-i-ten-tia-ry. I'm not in your town to stay, I will soon be on my way, I'm just here to get my ba-by out of jail. Yes war den, I'm just here to get my ba-by out of jail.

ARE YOU TIRED OF ME DARLING?

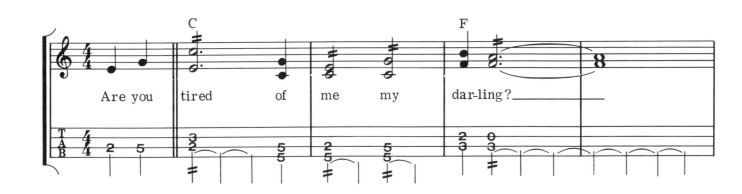

Are you tired of me my dar-ling?

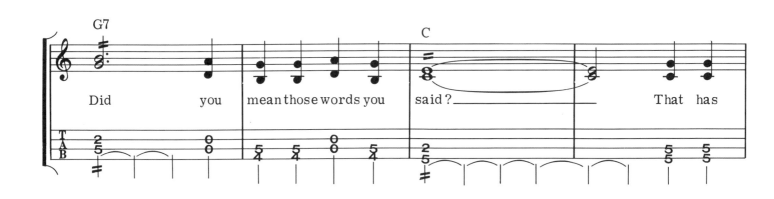

Did you mean those words you said?_____ That has

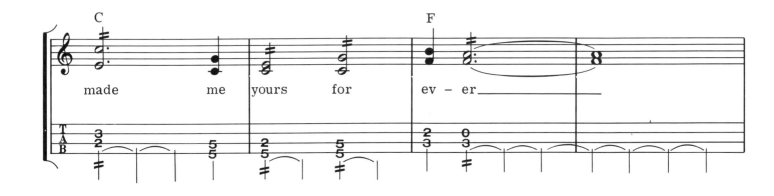

made me yours for ev – er_____

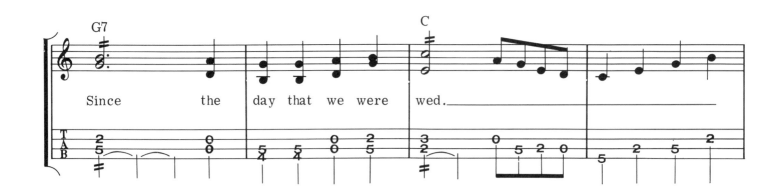

Since the day that we were wed._____

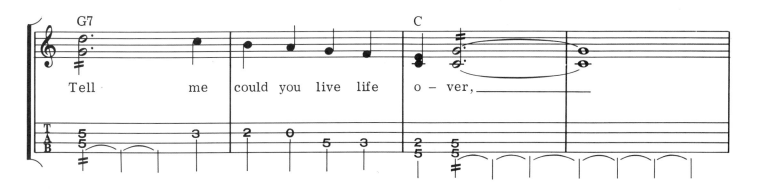

Tell me could you live life o - ver,

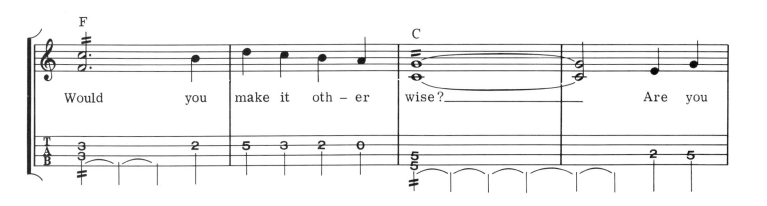

Would you make it oth - er wise? Are you

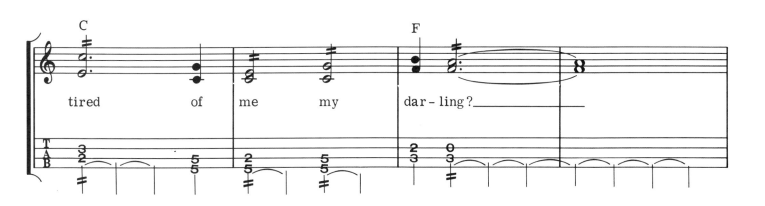

tired of me my dar - ling?

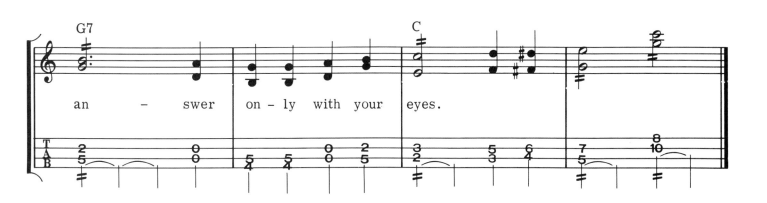

an - swer on - ly with your eyes.

113

KNOXVILLE GIRL

I met a lit-tle girl in Knox — ville, A

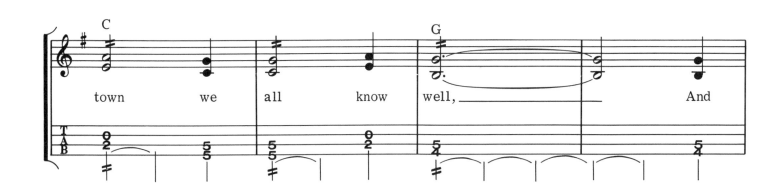

town we all know well,_____ And

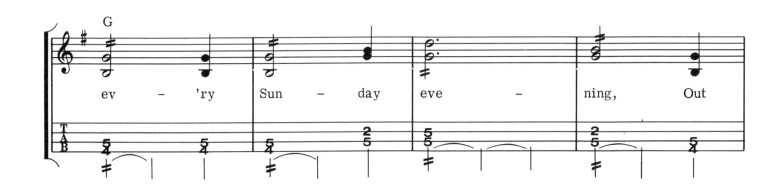

ev — 'ry Sun — day eve — ning, Out

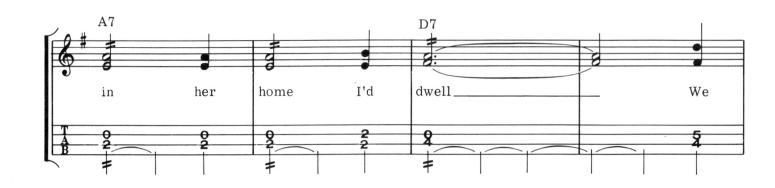

in her home I'd dwell_____ We

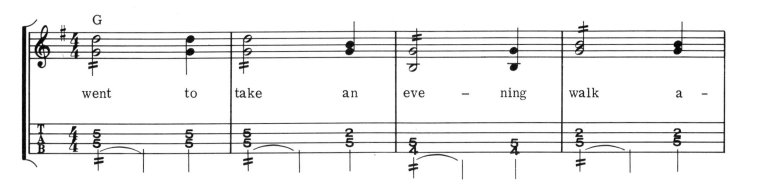

went to take an eve — ning walk a-

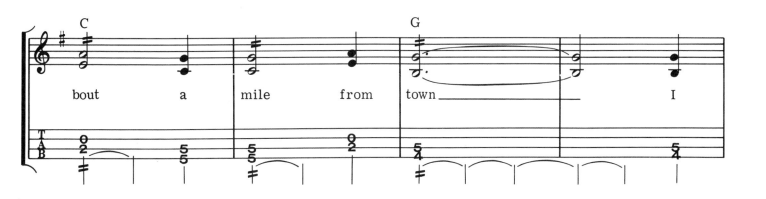

bout a mile from town_____ I

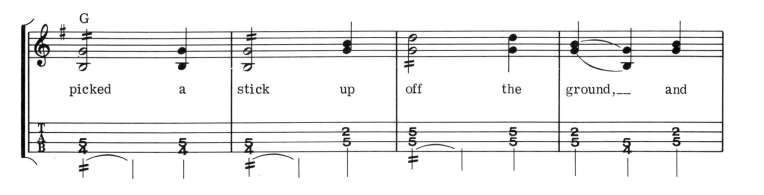

picked a stick up off the ground,___ and

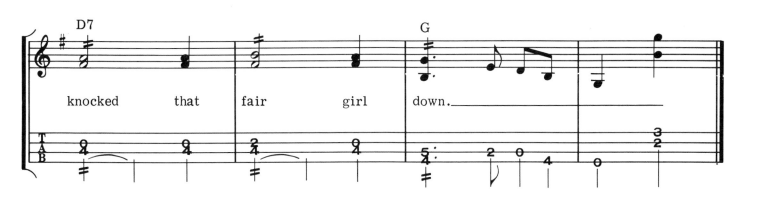

knocked that fair girl down._____

BURY ME BENEATH THE WILLOW

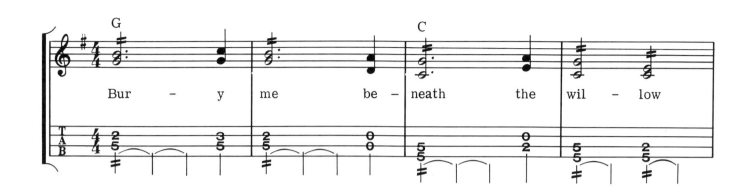

Bur - y me be - neath the wil - low

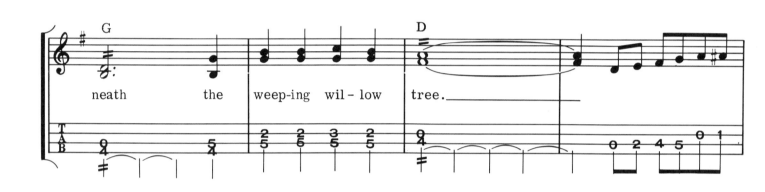

neath the weep-ing wil - low tree.____

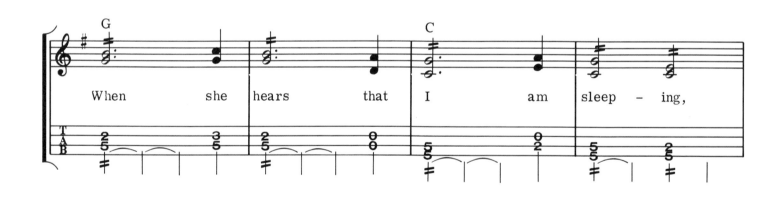

When she hears that I am sleep - ing,

may - be she will weep for me.____

WABASH CANNON BALL

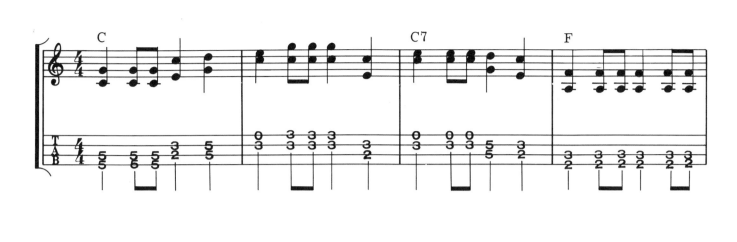

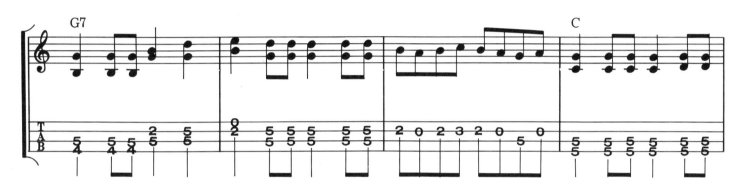

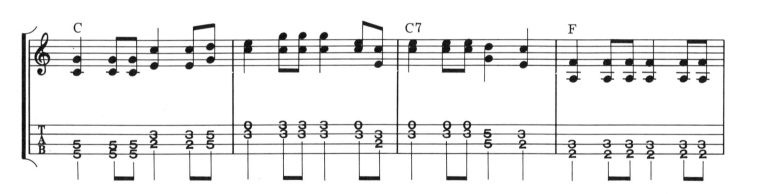

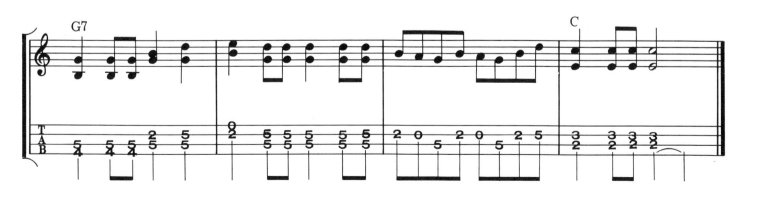

SITTIN ON TOP OF THE WORLD

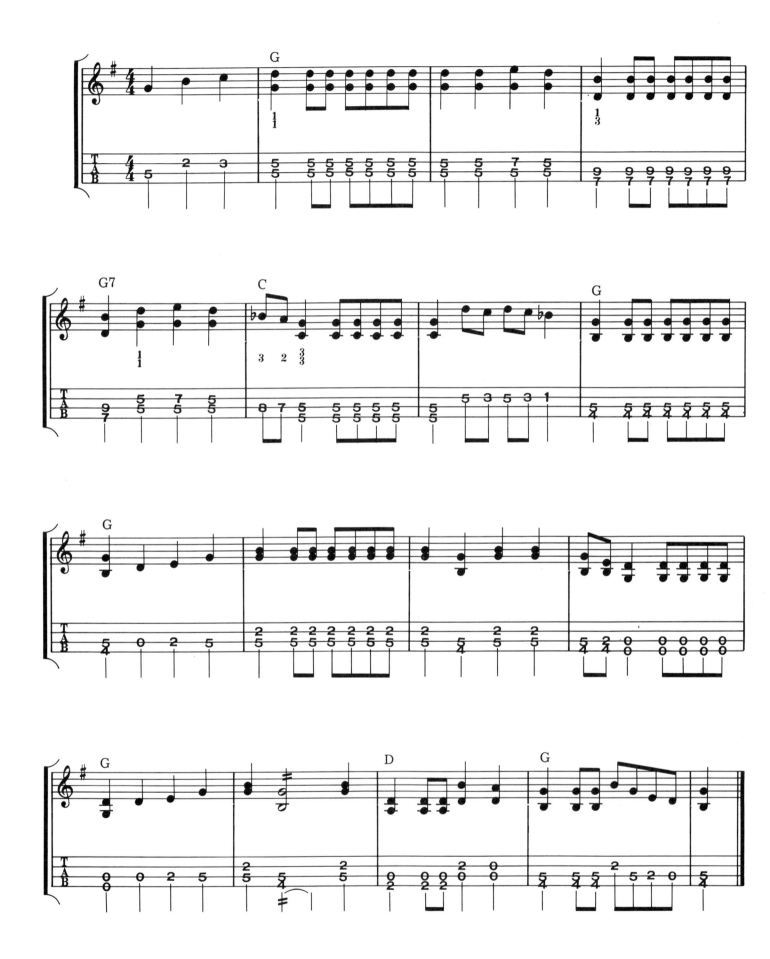

IN THE PINES

The long-est train I ev-er__ saw, Went__ down that__ Georg-ia__ line. The__ en-gine passed at six o'-clock, and the cab passed by at__ nine. In the pines, in the pines, where the sun nev-er shines, and we shiv-er when the cold wind__ blows._____

GRANDFATHER'S CLOCK

MANDOLIN FIESTA
(Easy Arrangement)

Bud Orr

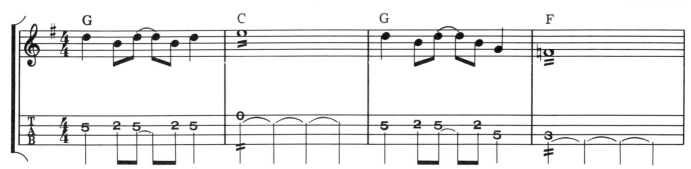

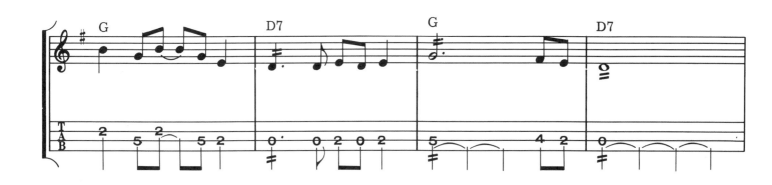

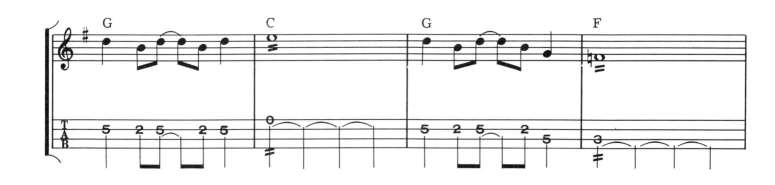

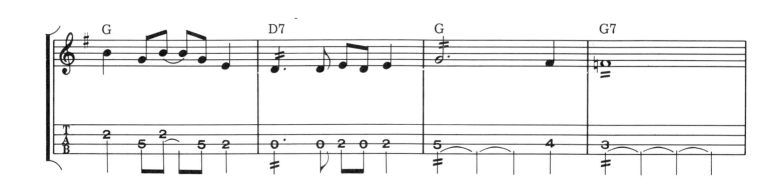

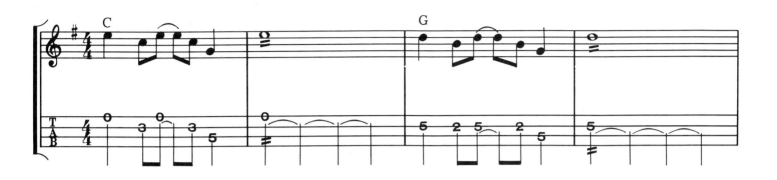

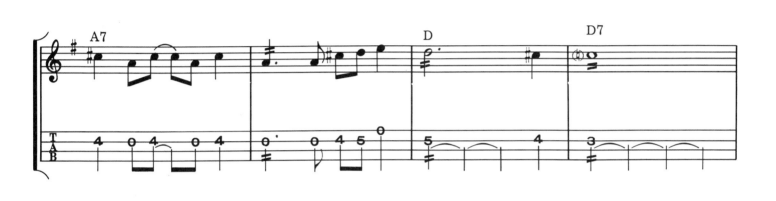

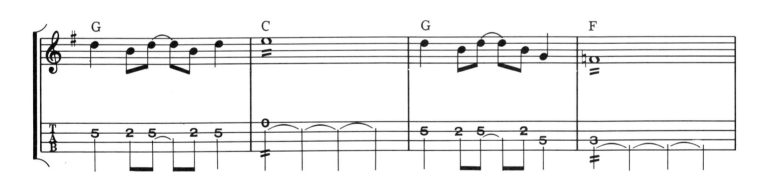

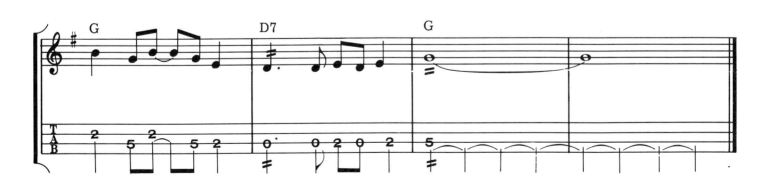

MANDOLIN FIESTA
(Mandolin Arrangement)

Bud Orr

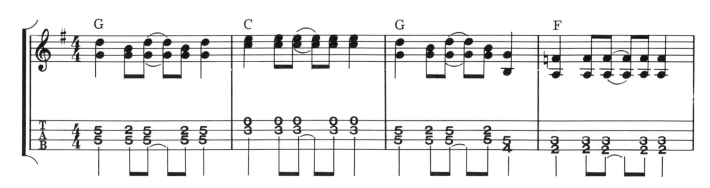

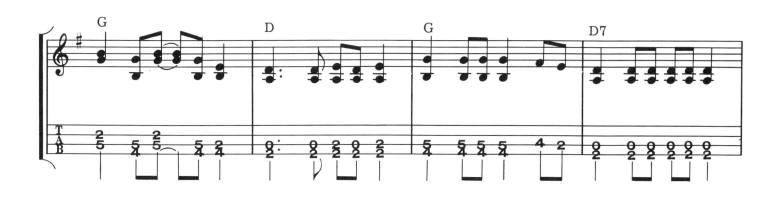

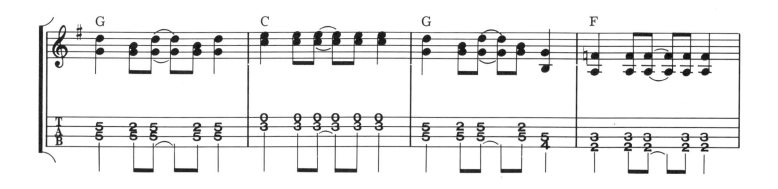

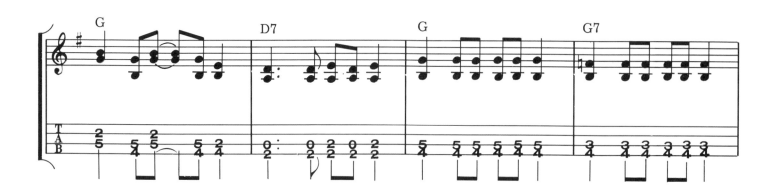

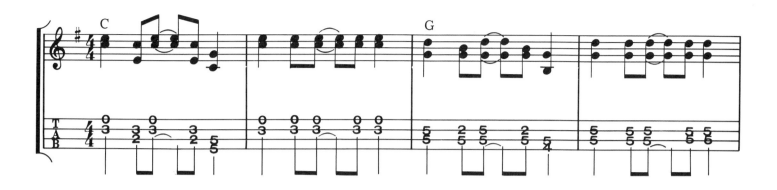

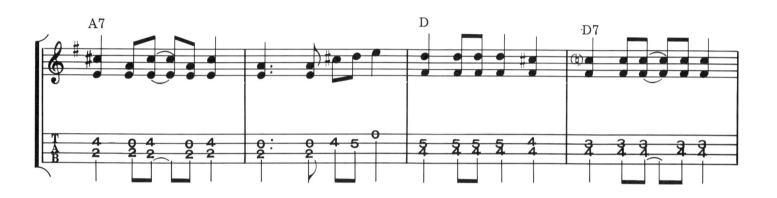

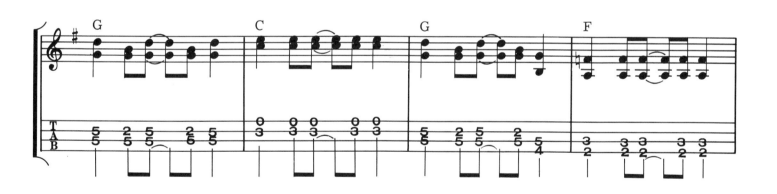

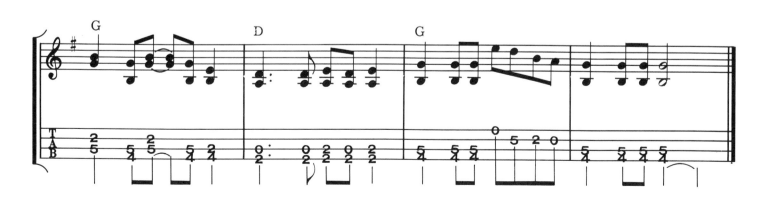

WILDWOOD FLOWER

NASHVILLE BLUES

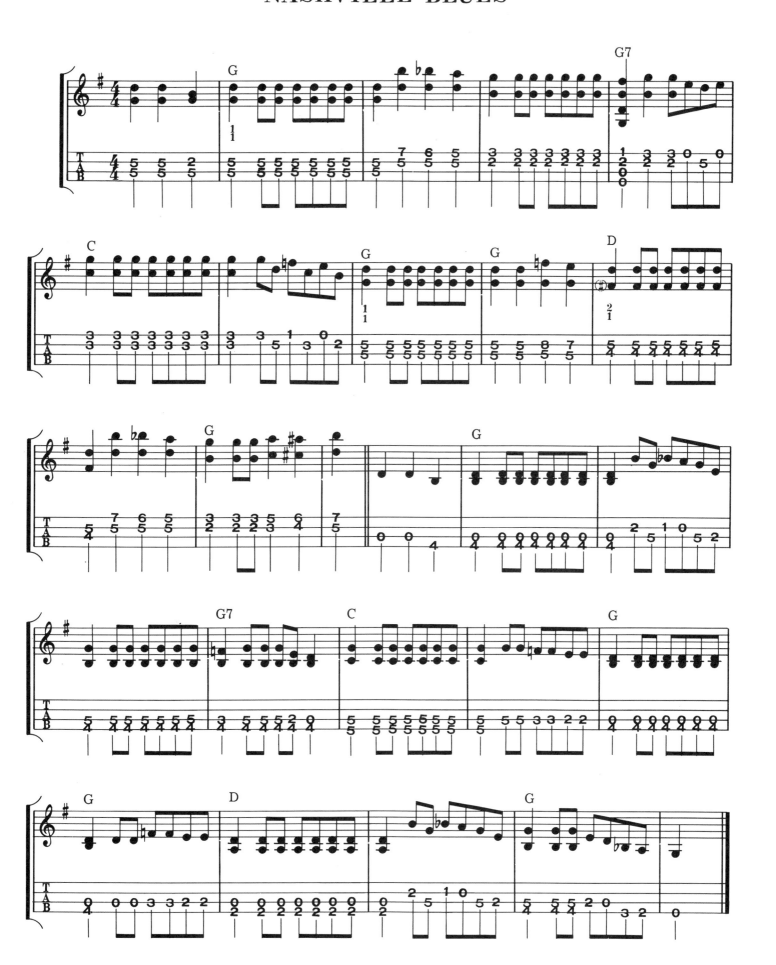

MY HOME'S ACROSS THE BLUE RIDGE MOUNTAINS

FIDDLE TYPE TUNE
MUSIC SECTION

IRISH WASHERWOMAN

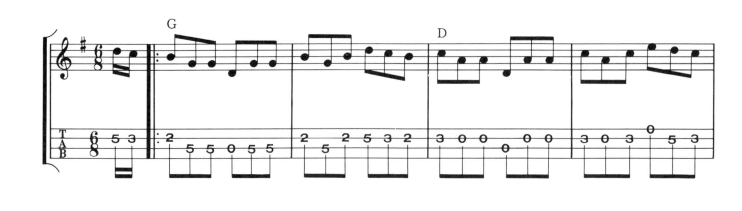

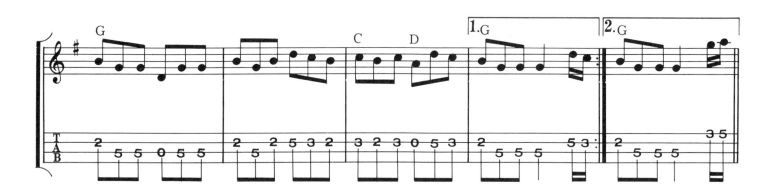

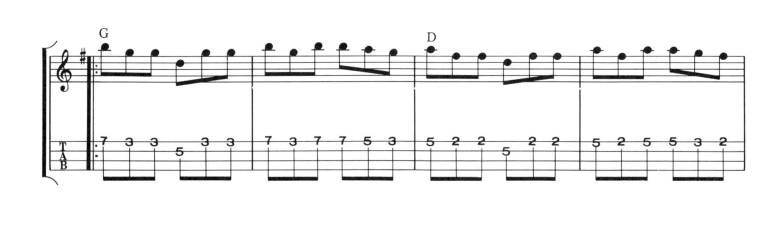

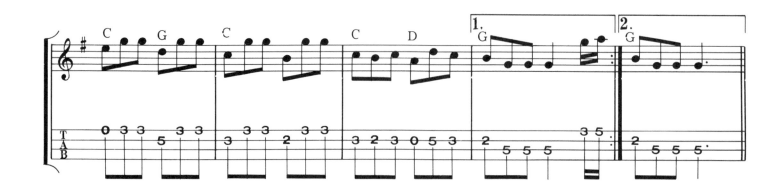

MANDOLIN BREAKDOWN

Bud Orr

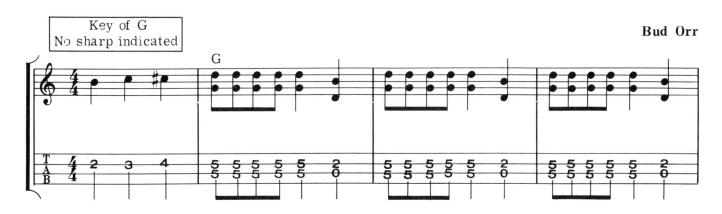

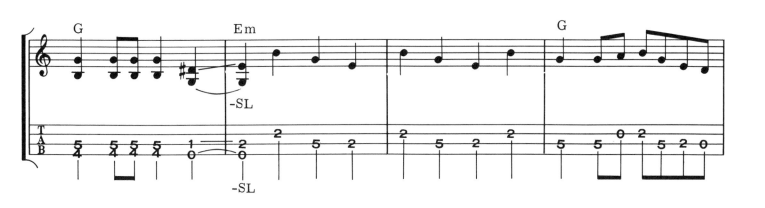

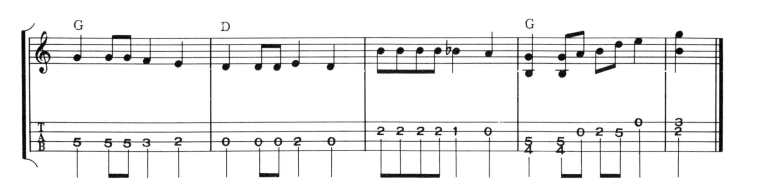

BLACKBERRY BLOSSOM
(Low Octave Version)

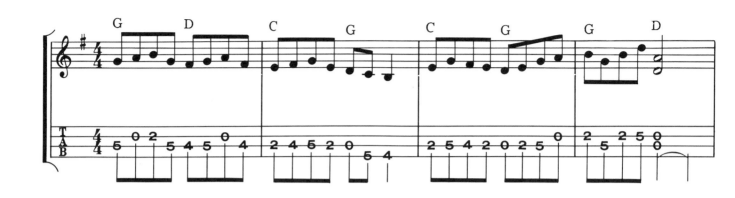

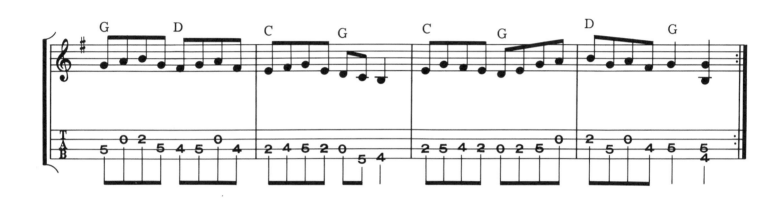

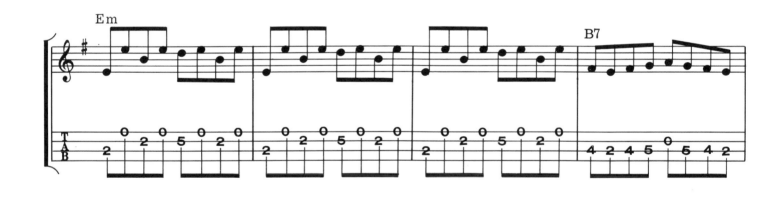

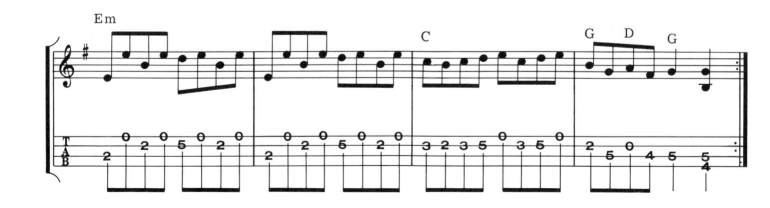

BLACKBERRY BLOSSOM
（High Octave Version）

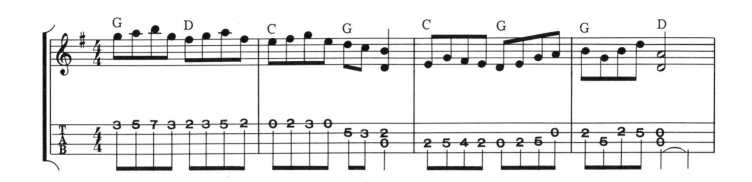

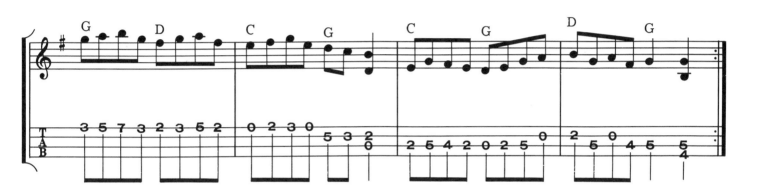

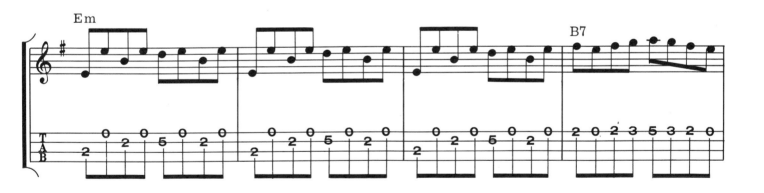

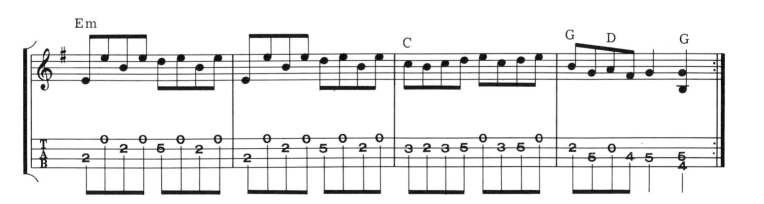

FISHER'S HORNPIPE

RICKETT'S HORNPIPE

SAILORS HORNPIPE

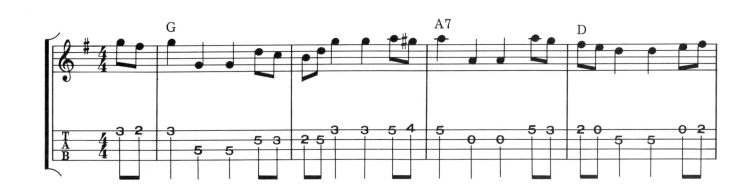

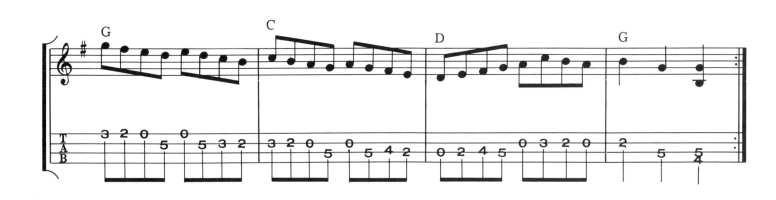

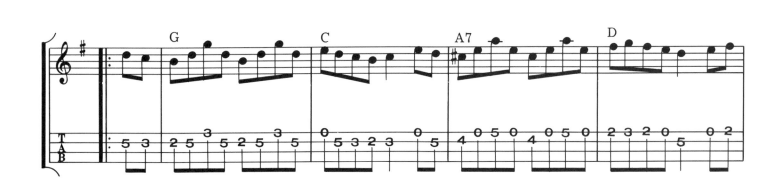

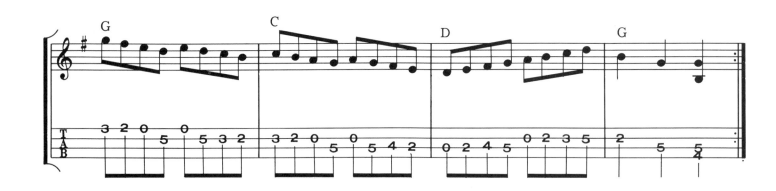

MISSISSIPPI SAWYER

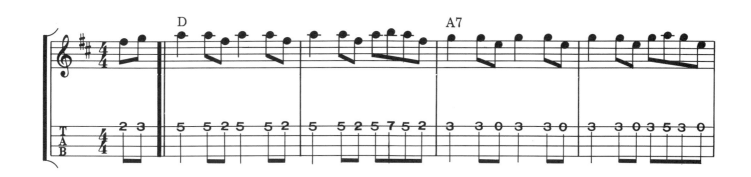

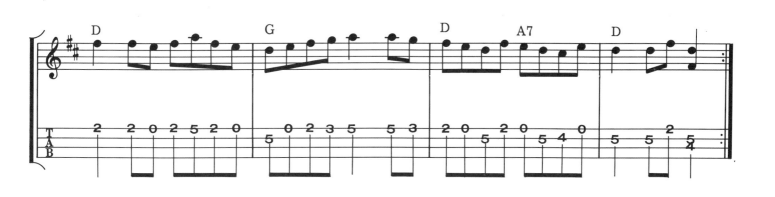

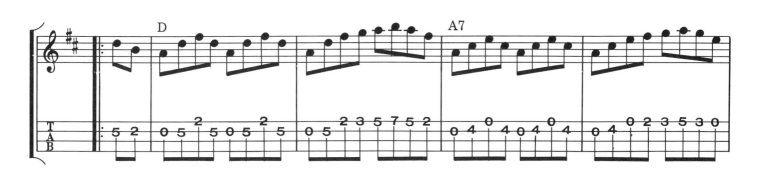

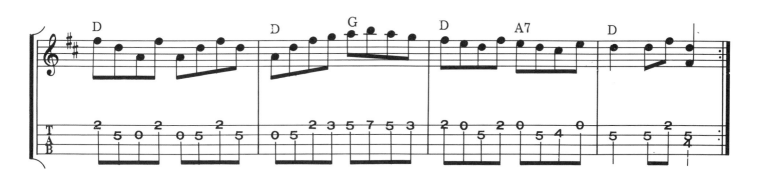

FLOP EARED MULE
(Low Octave Version)

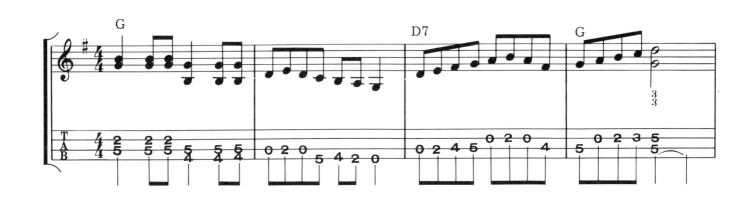

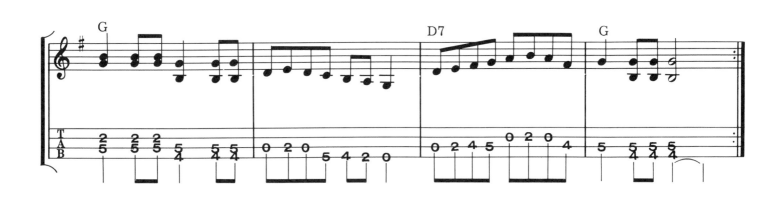

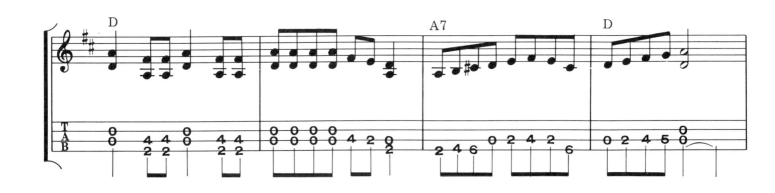

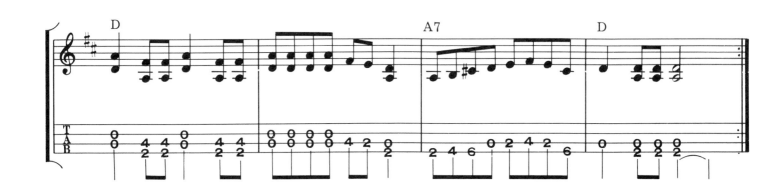

FLOP EARED MULE
(High Octave Version)

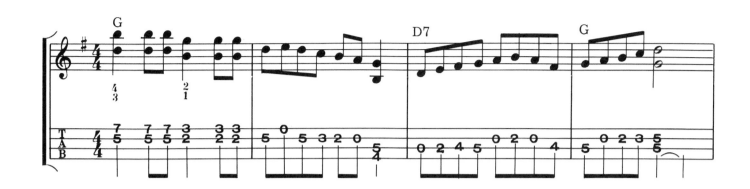

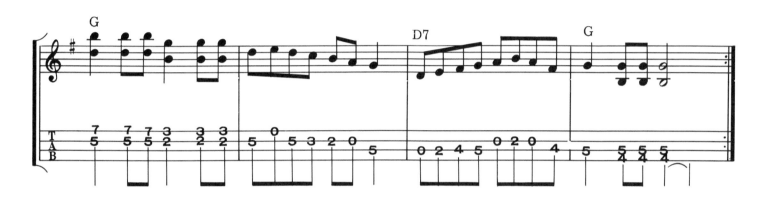

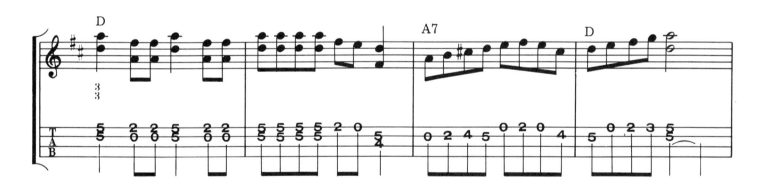

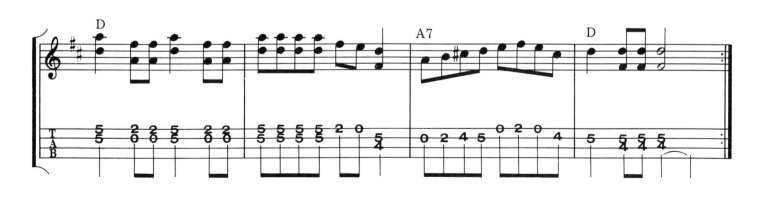

BILLY IN THE LOWGROUND

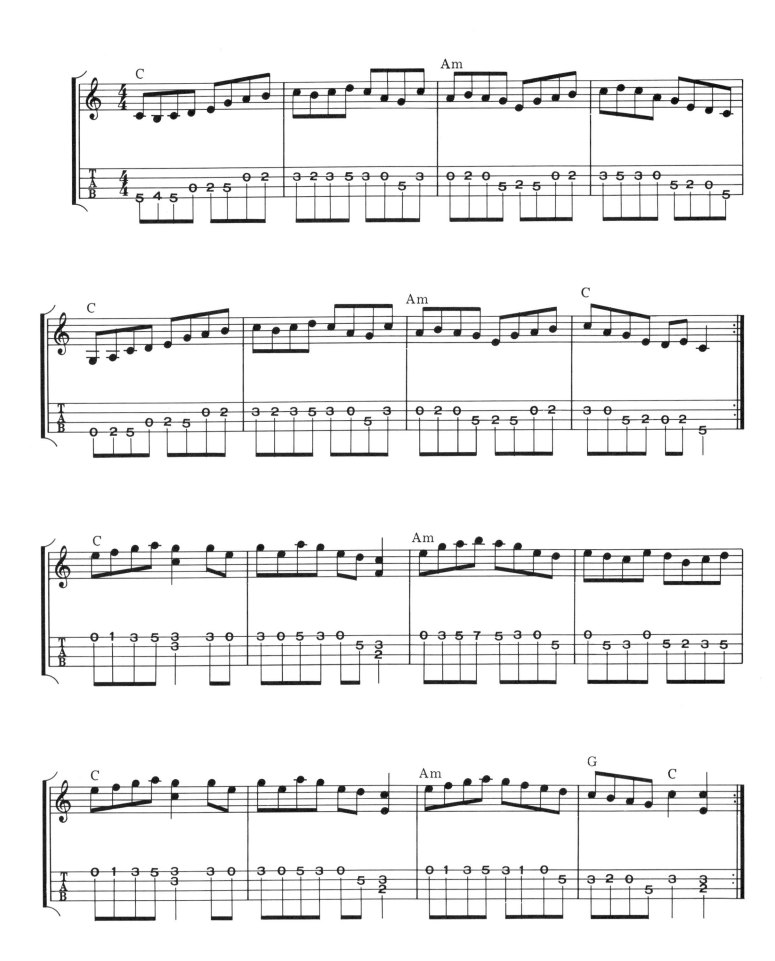

BALDHEADED END OF THE BROOM

BEAUMONT RAG

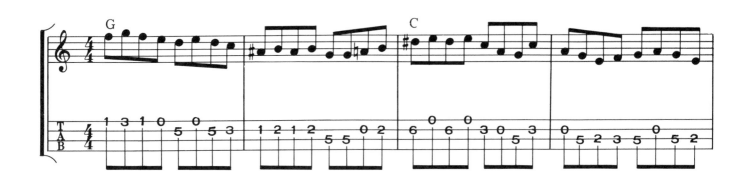

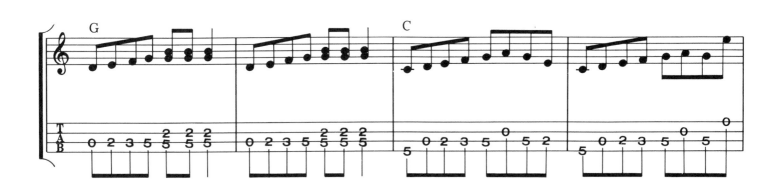

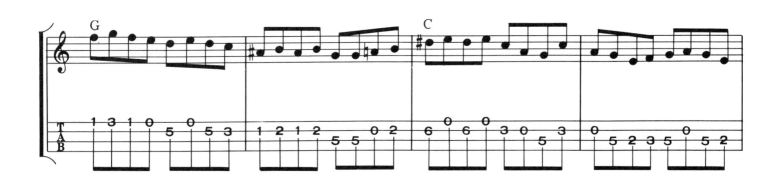

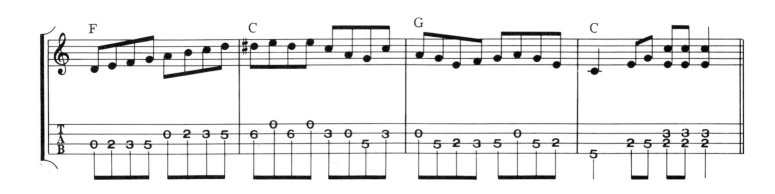

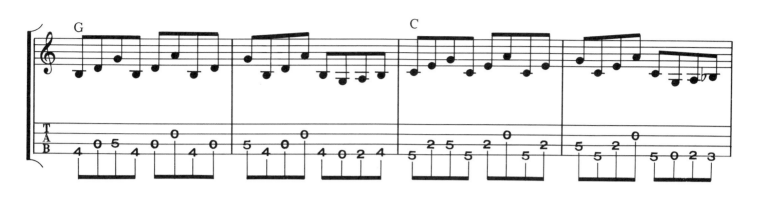

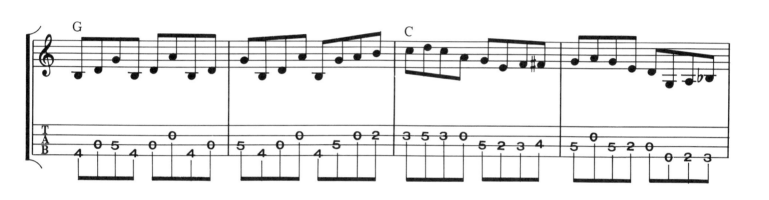

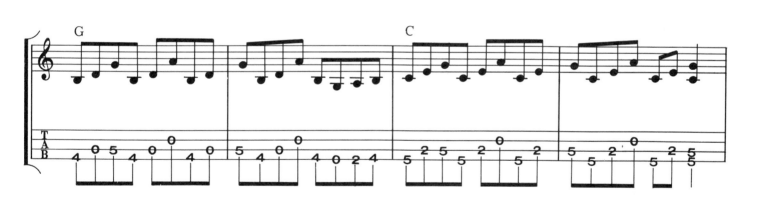

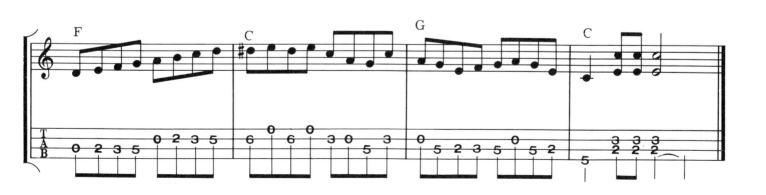

BACK UP AND PUSH

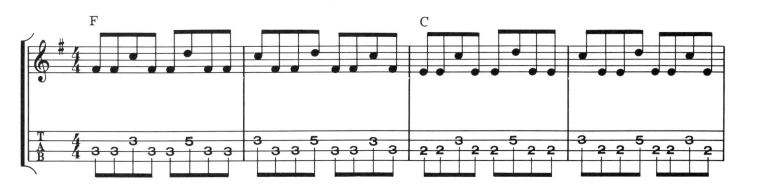

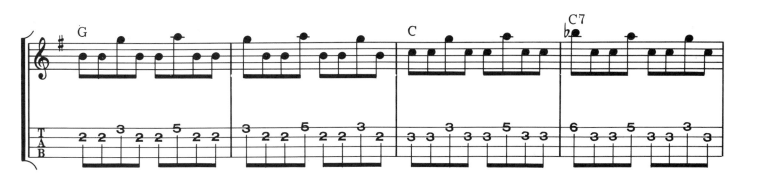

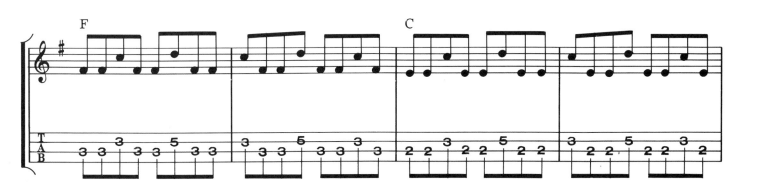

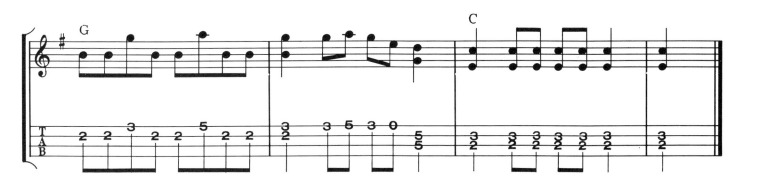

STOCKADE BLUES

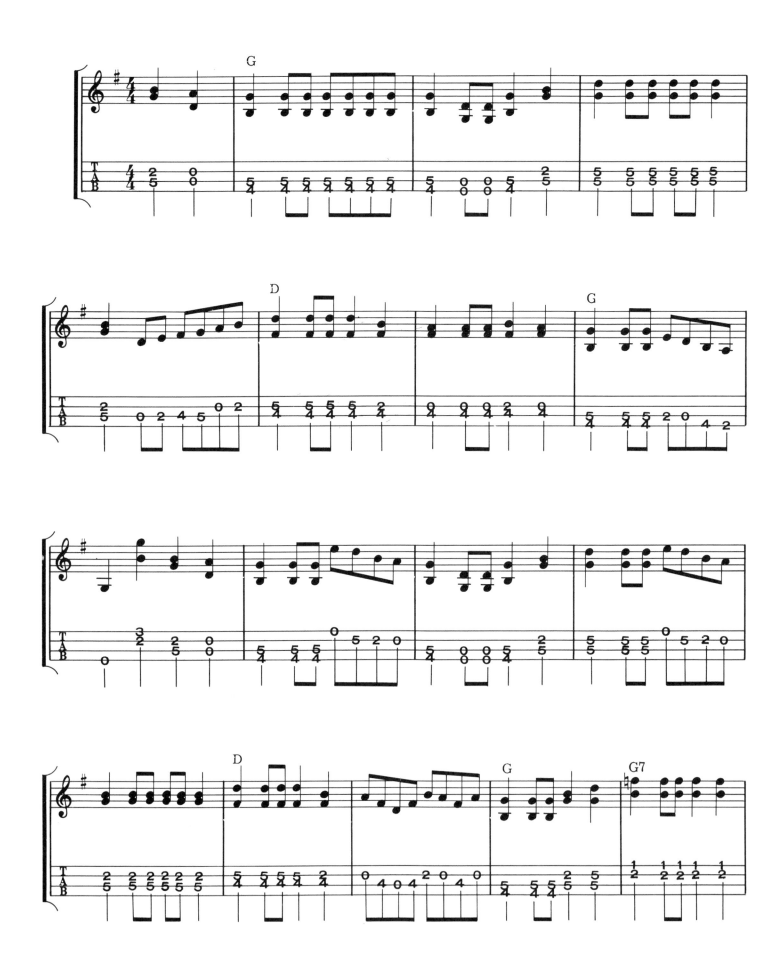

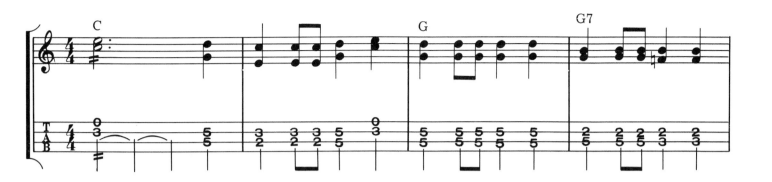

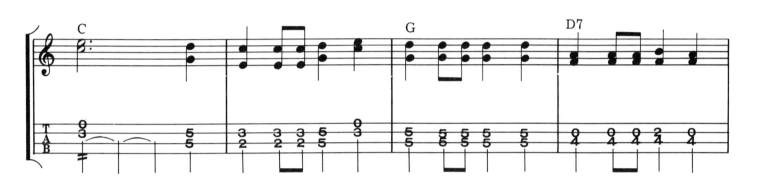

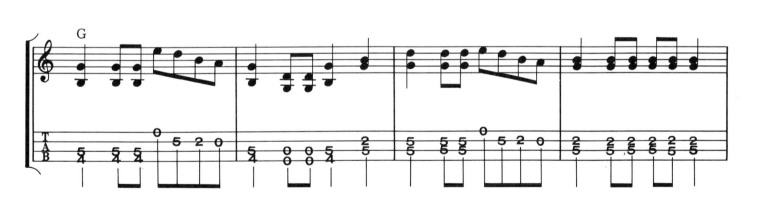

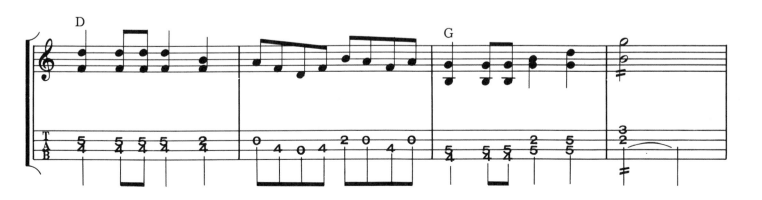

MISS McCLEOD'S REEL

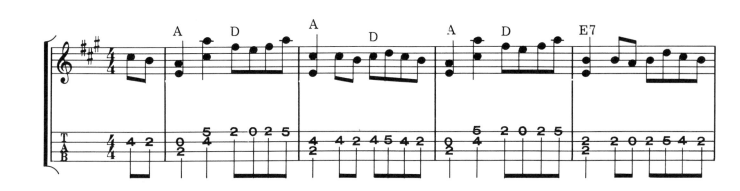

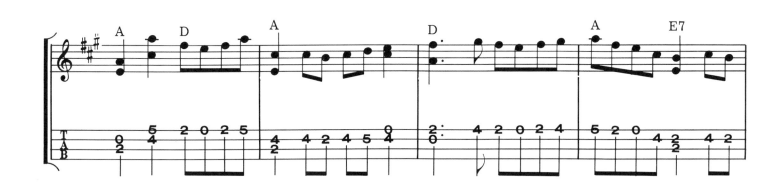

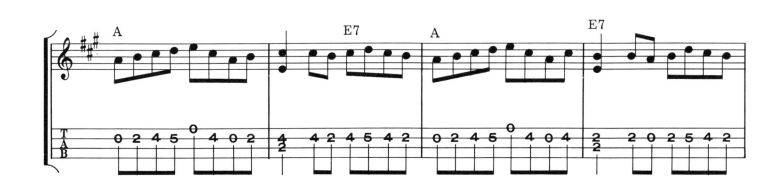

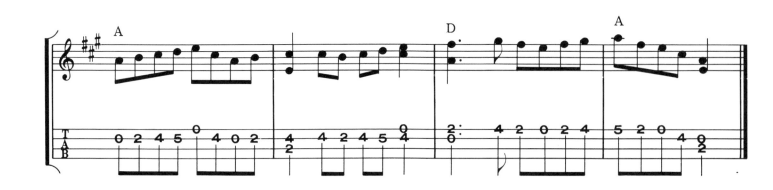

CHINESE BREAKDOWN

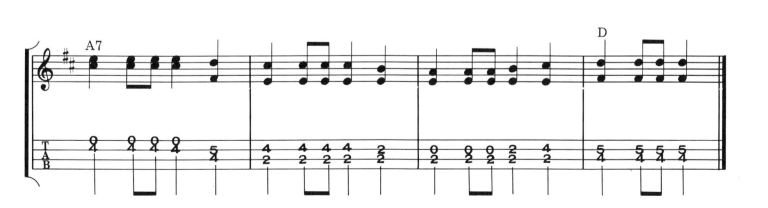

DOWN YONDER

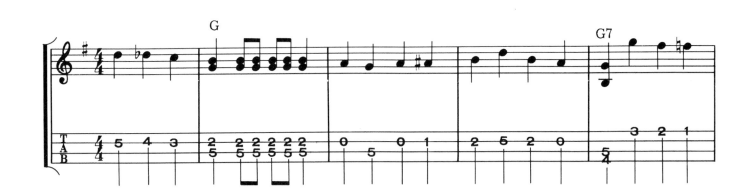

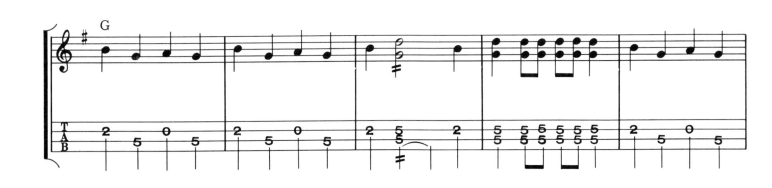

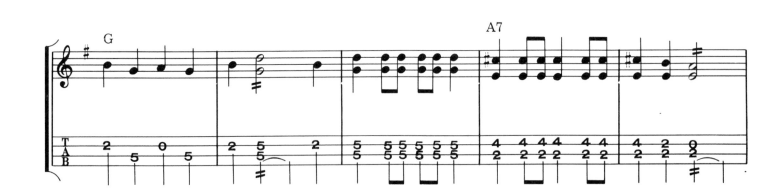

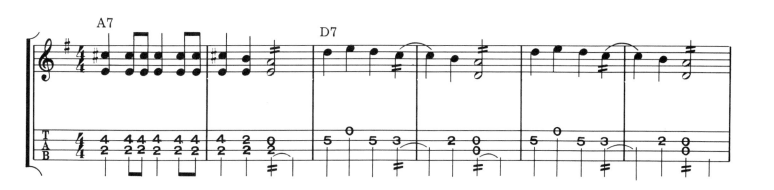

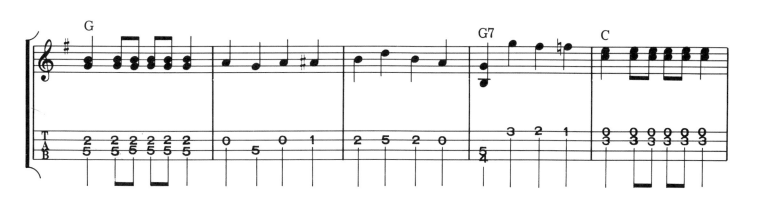

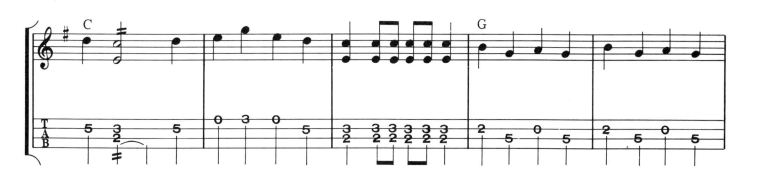

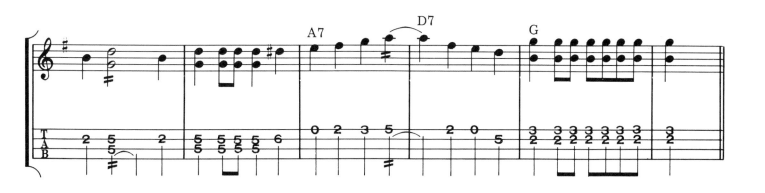

RED WING

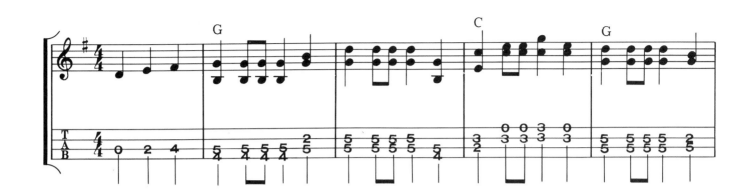

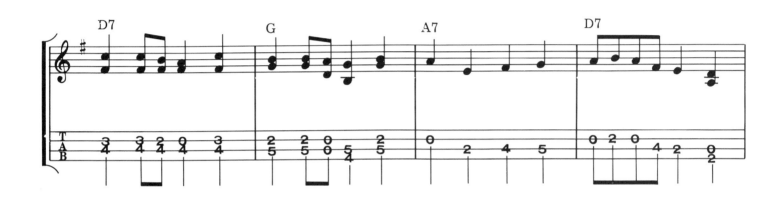

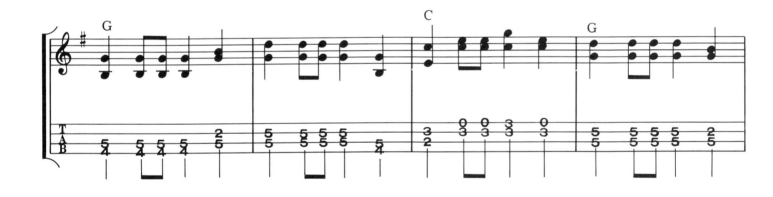

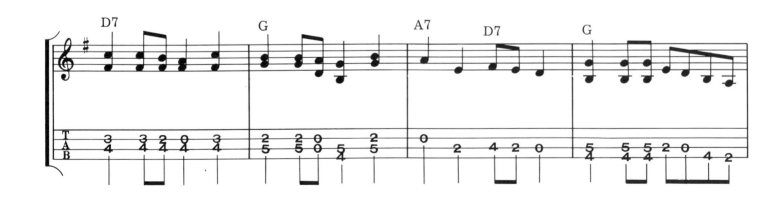

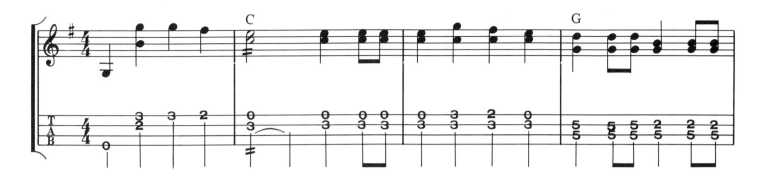

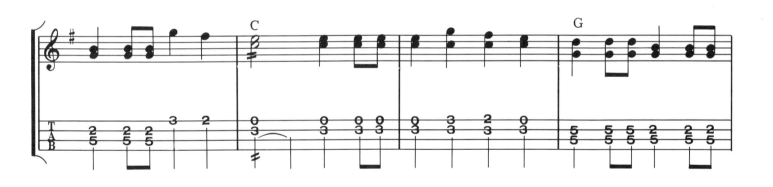

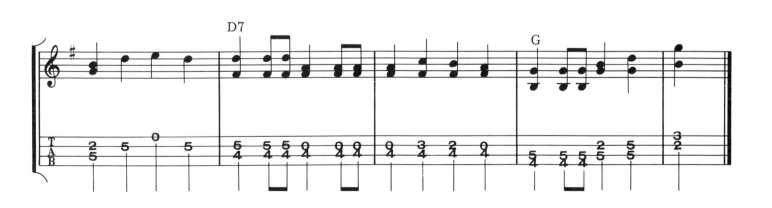

HOME, SWEET HOME

154

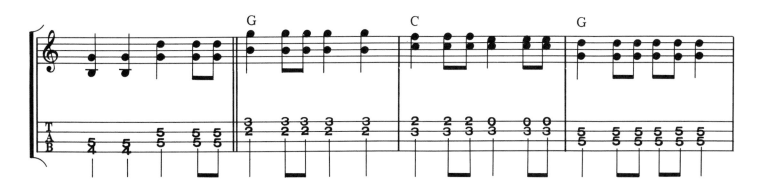
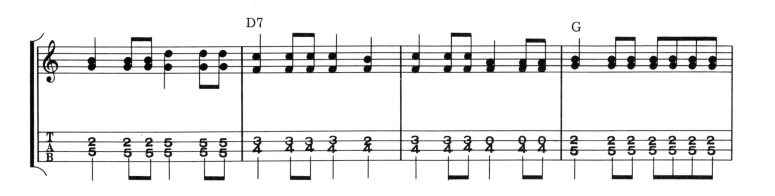
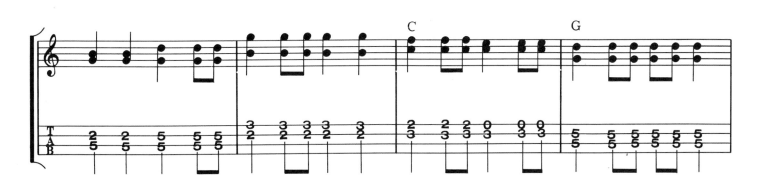
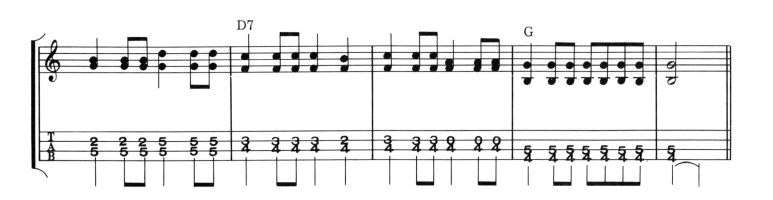

WAIT FOR THE WAGON

CINDY

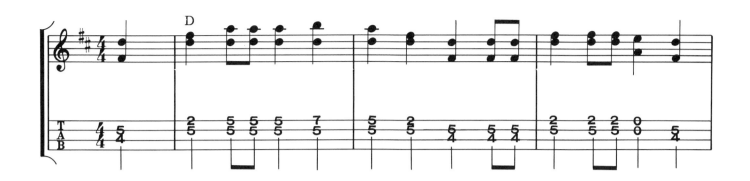

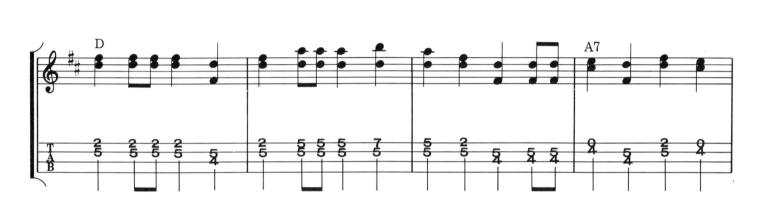

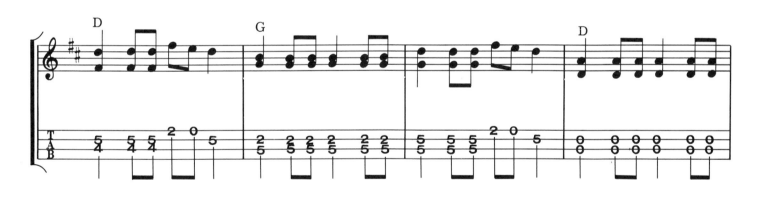

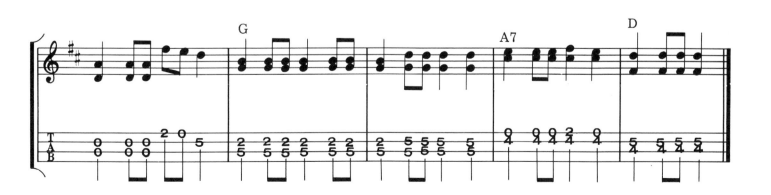

BUD'S BREAKDOWN

Bud Orr

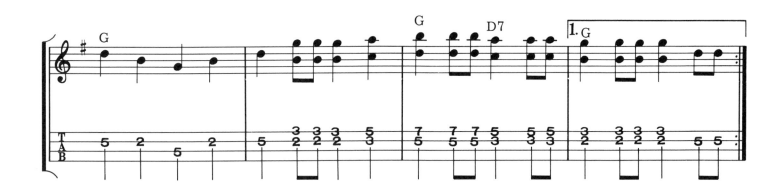

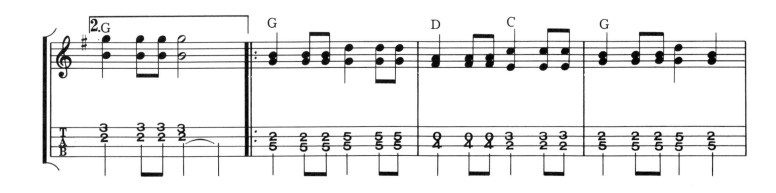

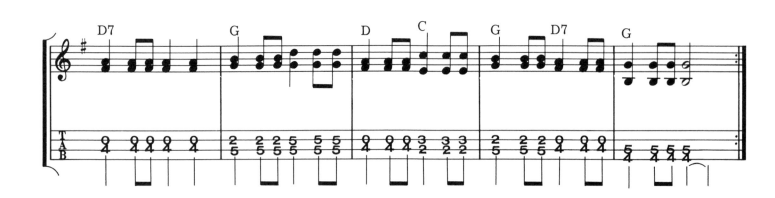

MOLLY PUT THE KETTLE ON

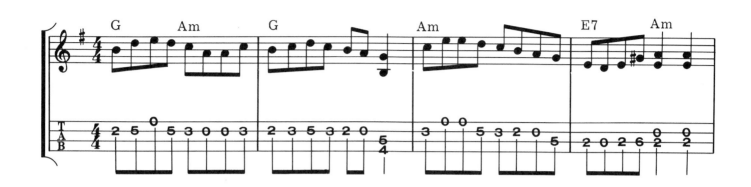

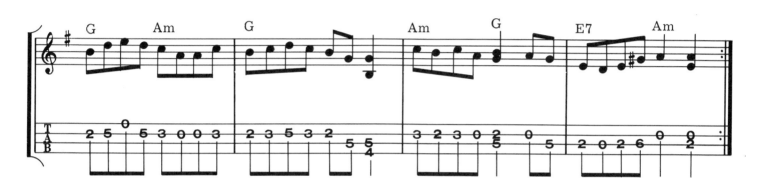

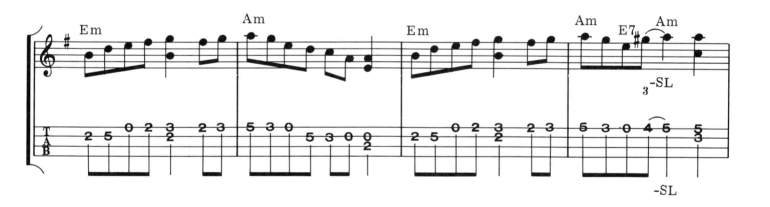

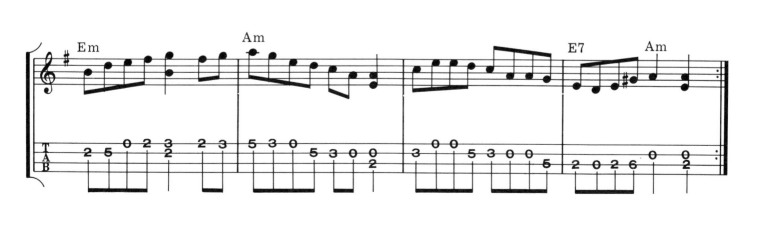

THE GREEN FIELDS OF AMERICA

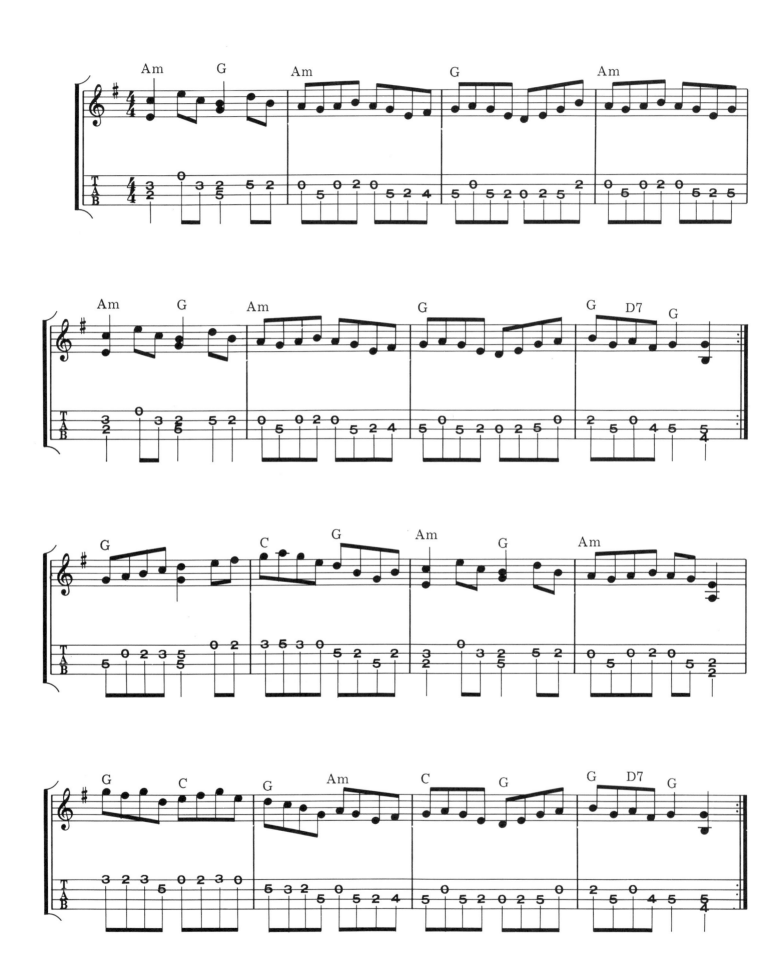

GOODBYE LIZA JANE

161

OVER THE WATERFALL

Mandolin

GARRY OWEN
(Jig)

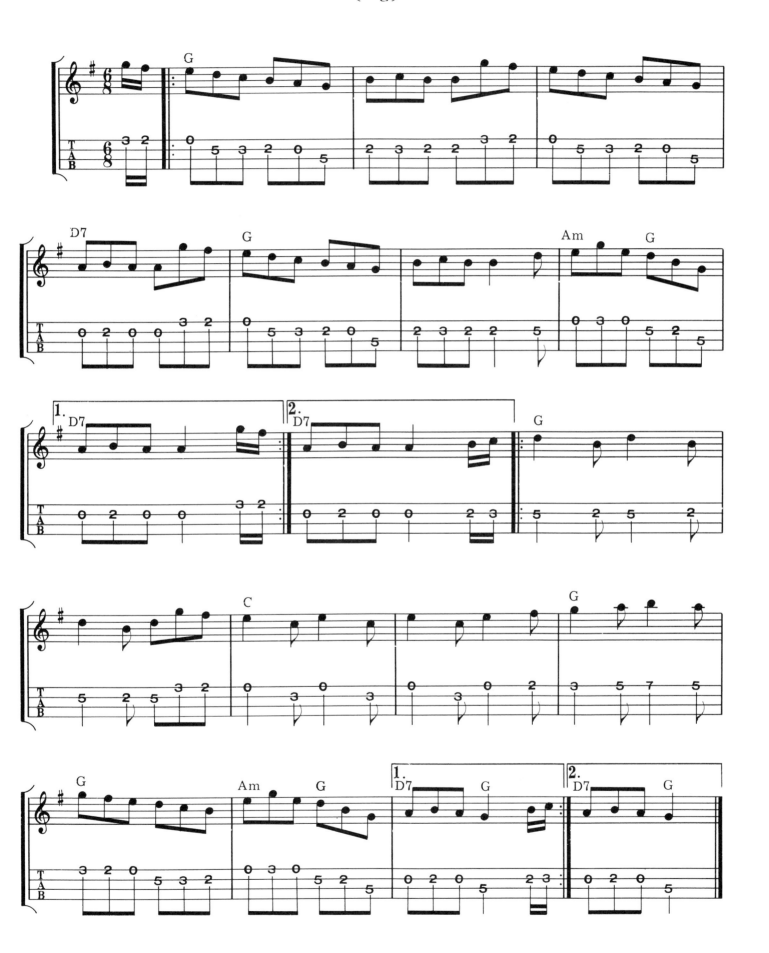

DUXBURY HORNPIPE

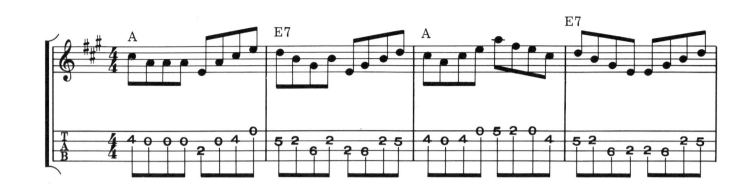

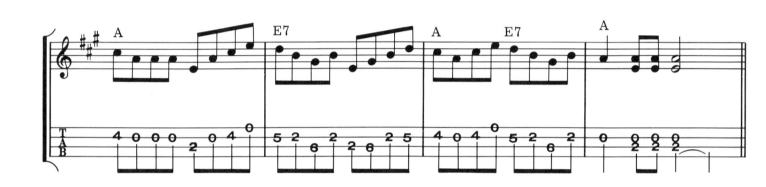

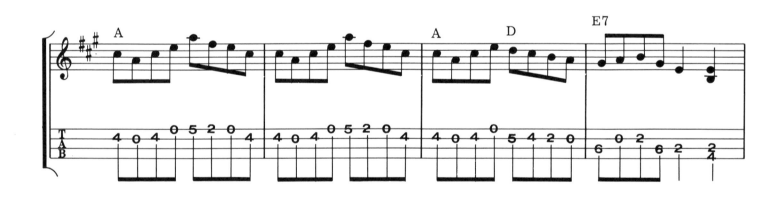

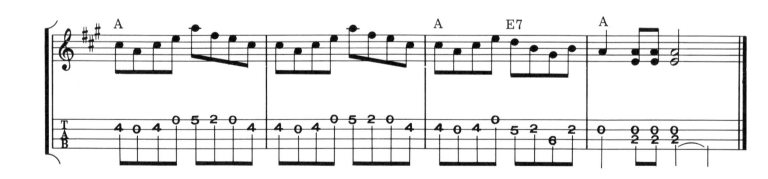

RED HAIRED BOY

SALTY DOG

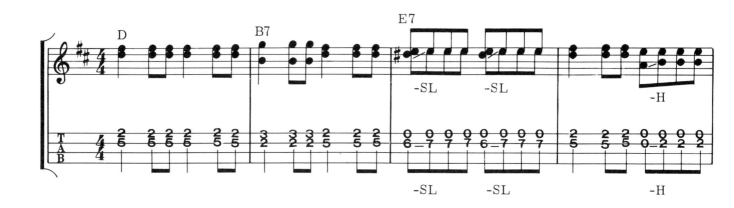

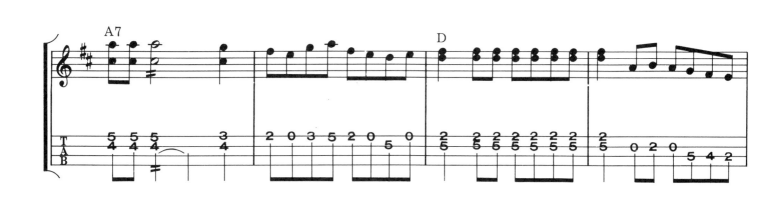

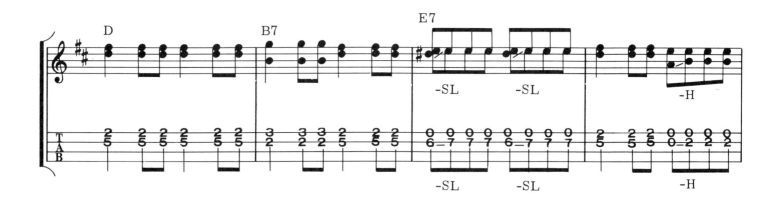

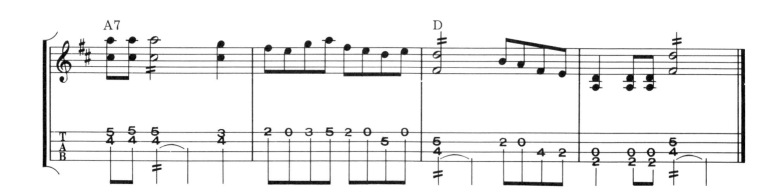

DIXIELAND AND RAG
MUSIC SECTION

BILL BAILEY

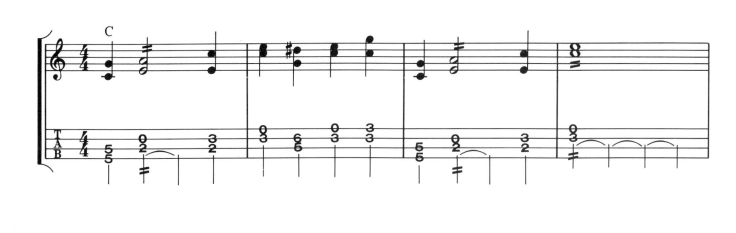

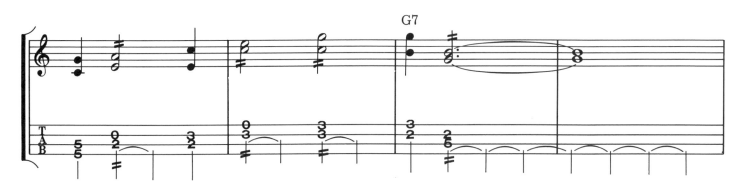

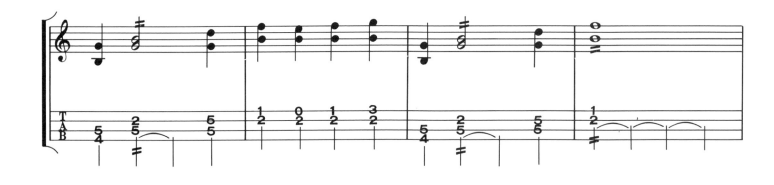

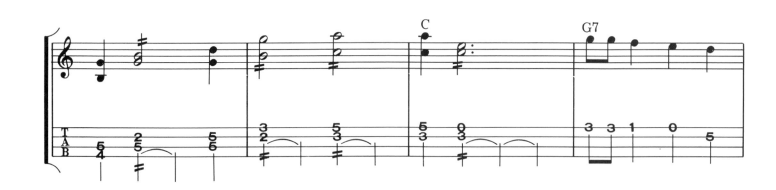

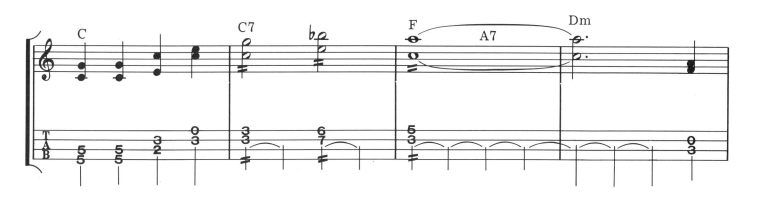

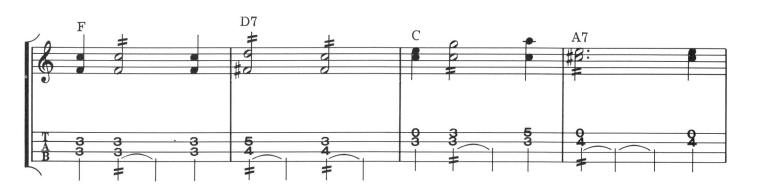

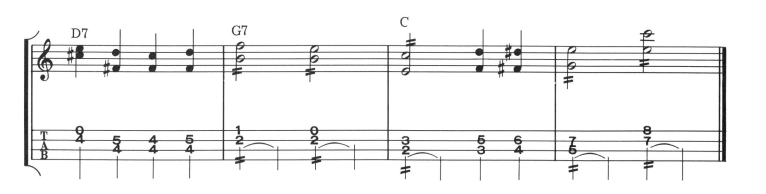

WAIT TILL THE SUN SHINES NELLY

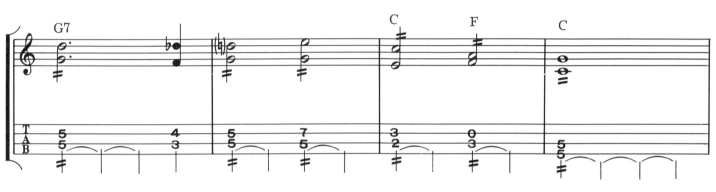

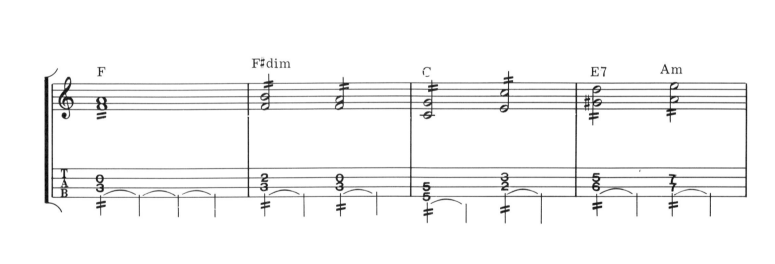

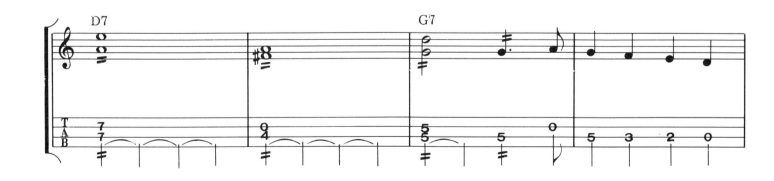

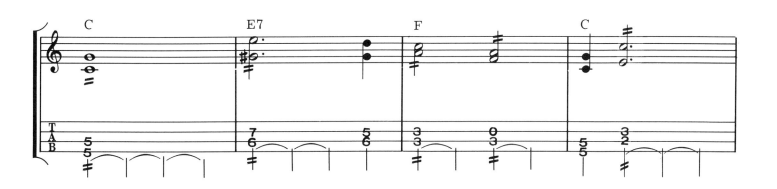

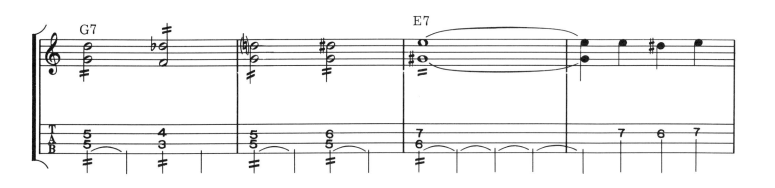

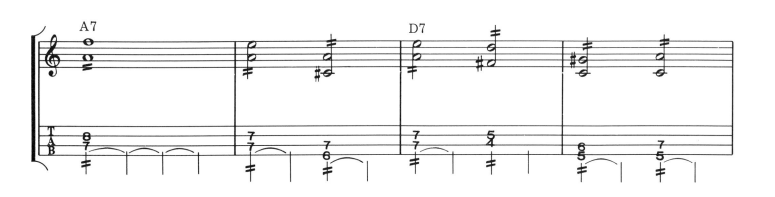

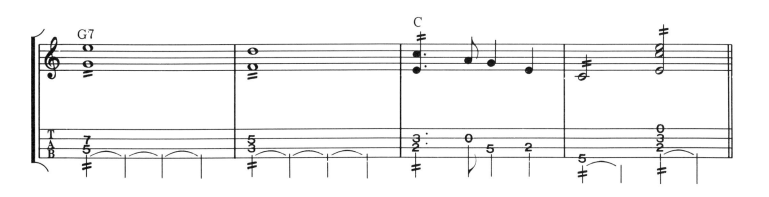

FAREWELL BLUES

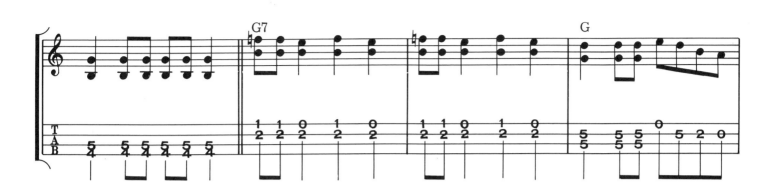

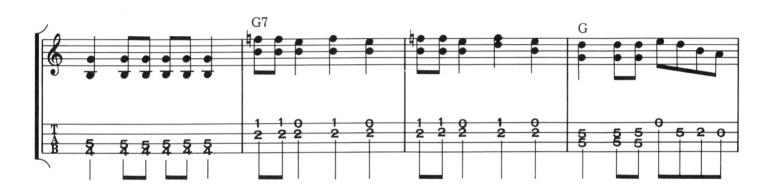

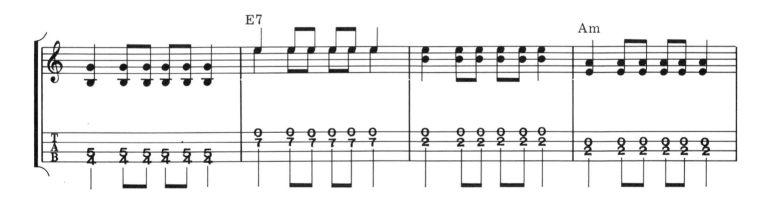

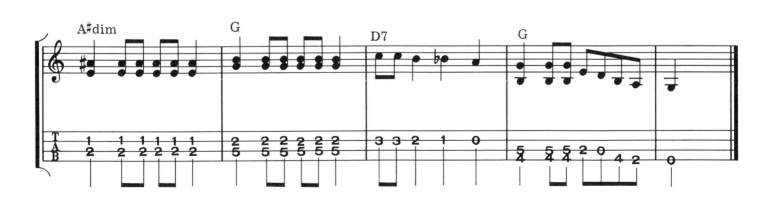

WHEN THE SAINTS GO MARCHING IN

BUD'S MANDOLIN RAG

Bud Orr

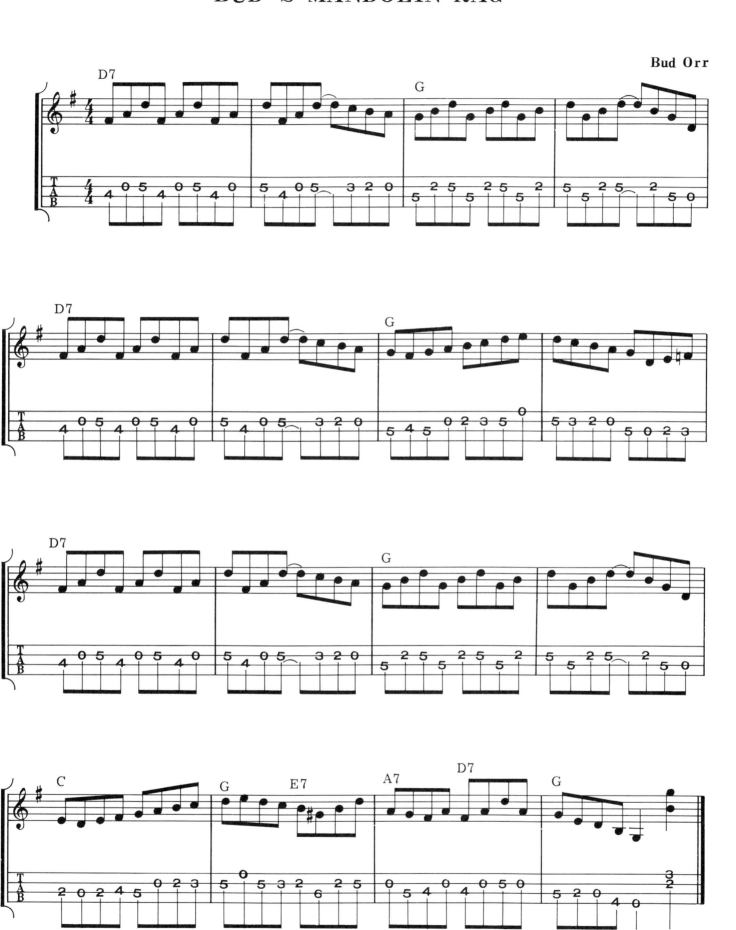

STONE'S RAG

PENTATONIC SCALE STUDY

The major pentatonic scale consists of only five notes taken from the major scale of the same name. As shown in the example below, a pentatonic scale is derived by using the 1st, 2nd, 3rd, 5th and 6th notes of a major scale omitting the 4th and 7th notes.

This scale is used very extensively by country and bluegrass musicians for improvising. In playing in the key of G major, variations of notes from this scale can be used over chords most commonly found. (G, C, D, Em, Am and Dm)

Scale tones	1	2	3	4	5	6	7	8
G major scale	G	A	B	C	D	E	F♯	G
G pentatonic scale	G	A	B		D	E		G

G major scale

G pentatonic scale

Study and play these scale patterns to songs that you know in the key of G major until you have thoroughly memorized every note and can play them fluently. After this is accomplished practice using different rhythms; quarter notes, dotted quarter notes, eighth notes, etc. Do not just use scales and patterns. Improvise as melodically as possible and soon you'll discover many new ideas.

G Pentatonic scale

C Pentatonic scale

D Pentatonic scale

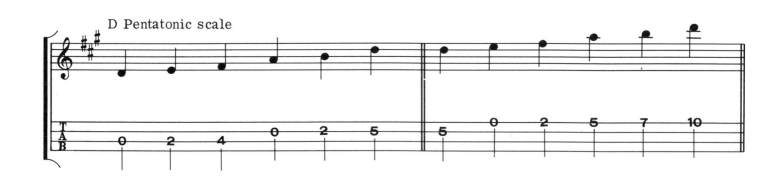

Note: In the scales shown above combined pentatonics include; G A B C D E F♯ G. All notes in the G major scale.

BILE DEM CABBAGE DOWN
(Melody)

Pentatonic Variation Number 1

Pentatonic Variation Number 2

A pentatonic scale

B pentatonic scale

E pentatonic scale

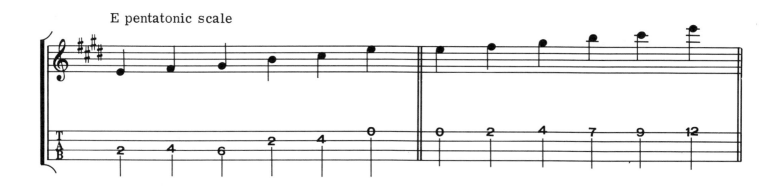

F pentatonic scale

MOVABLE PENTATONIC SCALES

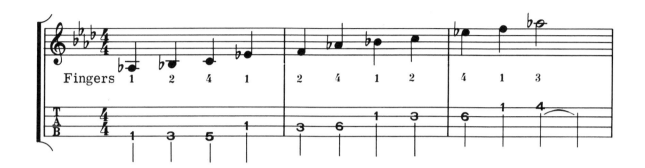

Sequence of notes

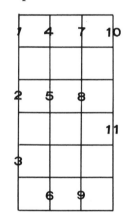

Fret	Key
1	G# or A♭
2	A
3	A# or B♭
4	B
5	C
6	C# or D♭
7	D
8	D# or E♭
9	E
10	F
11	F# or G♭
12	G

Fingers

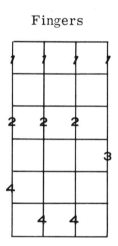

TWIN MANDOLIN STUDY

Harmony parts for two or three mandolins or a combination of mandolin, guitar, banjo or fiddle is very effective giving a full and beautiful sound. It can easily be compared to duet, trio, and quartet vocal parts. Writing or playing two or more parts is a relatively simple process with a basic understanding of music theory.

Chord Study

A major chord is built from the 1st, 3rd and 5th tone from the major scale. Example of a G major scale and how the chord is built:

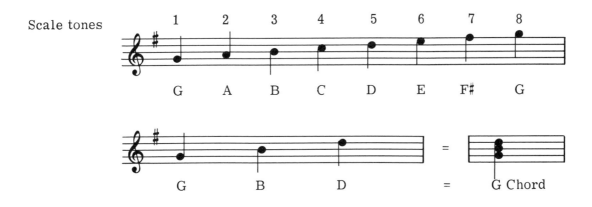

The chord tones in the harmony line are derived from the chord progression of the melody line.

Shown below are three arpeggios for the G, C and D chords. Arpeggios are one note played at a time from any given chord.

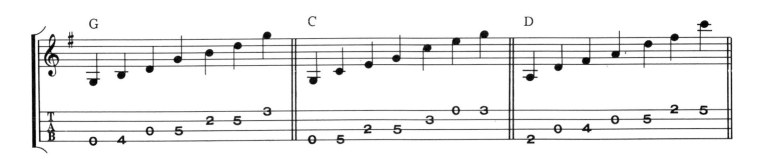

In this book all arrangements are written with the harmony below the melody. In vocal arrangements this is referred to as the baritone part. The harmony may also be written above the melody. In vocal arrangements this is the tenor part. Harmony for three instruments should be written and played with a part above and below the melody.

With a complete knowledge of the information shown on this page refer to the scales and transposition section in this book before attempting harmony parts in other keys.

BILE DEM CABBAGE DOWN
(1st Part) (Melody)

(2nd Part) (High)

(3rd Part) (Low)

CROSSPICKING

Crosspicking is basically playing a banjo style roll with a flat pick. This style may be used very effectively on the mandolin for playing back up or lead.

Shown below are three examples of crosspicking. The first is a backward roll which seems to be more popular with mandolin players. The second and third rolls are forward rolls. The only difference in the forward rolls is the picking directions.

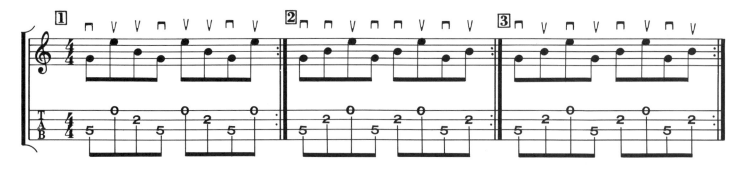

ARPEGGIOS FOR BACK UP

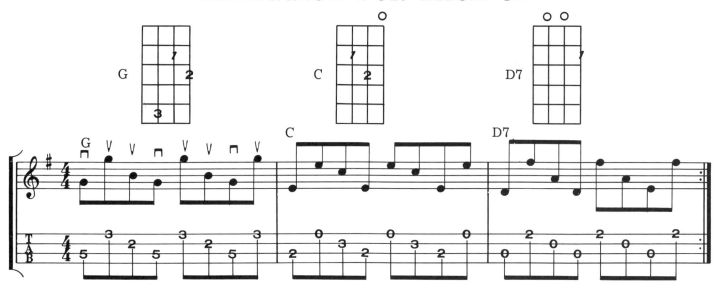

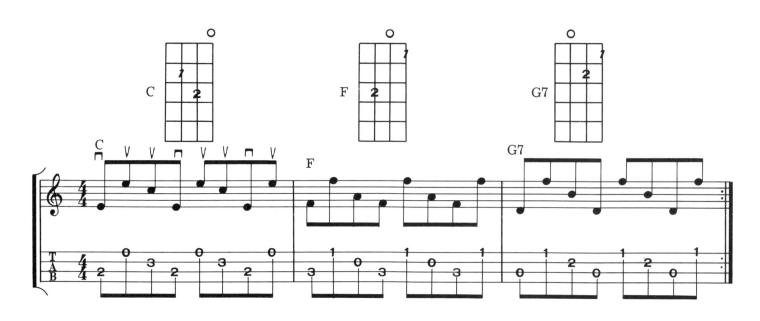

BILE DEM CABBAGE DOWN
(Crosspicking - Lead Pattern)

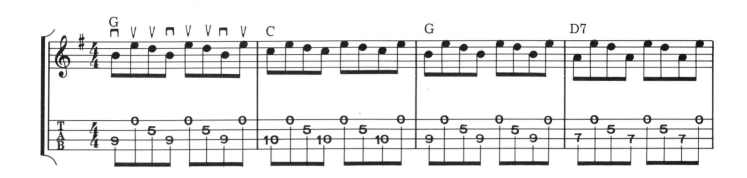

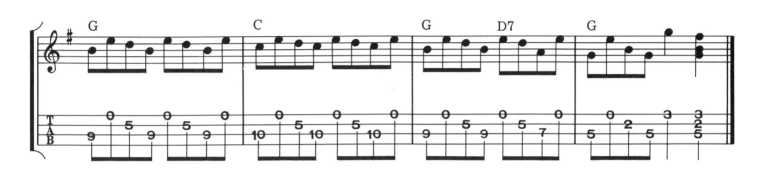

BILE DEM CABBAGE DOWN
(Crosspicking Improvisation)

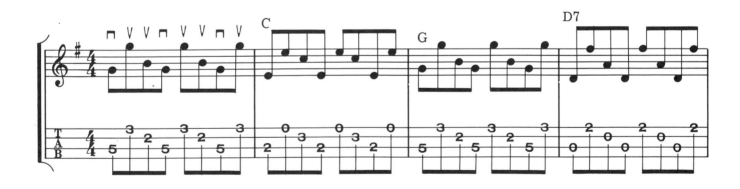

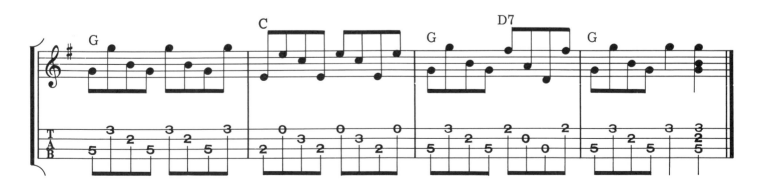

CROSS COUNTRY PICKIN'

Bud Orr

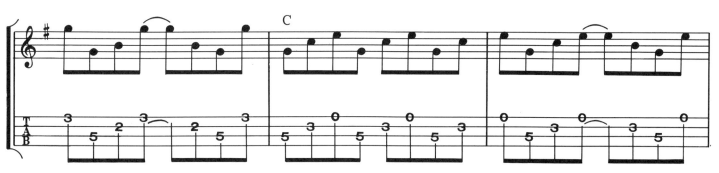

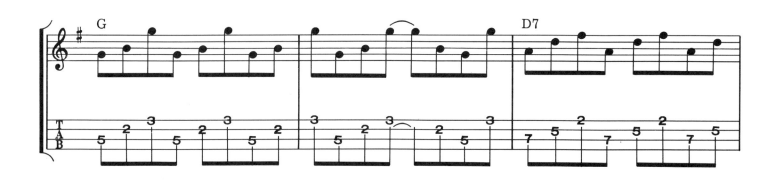

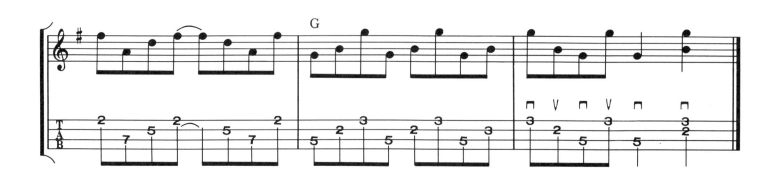

ROCK AND BLUES SECTION

MUSIC

STUDIES FOR ROCK AND BLUES

MUSIC

ROCKIN' EASY

Bud Orr

BUD'S MANDOLIN BOUNCE

Bud Orr

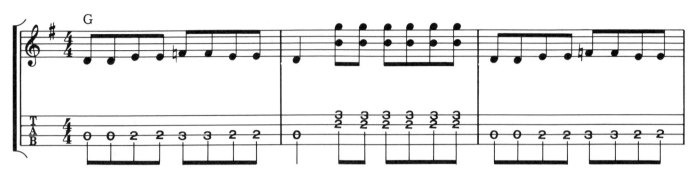

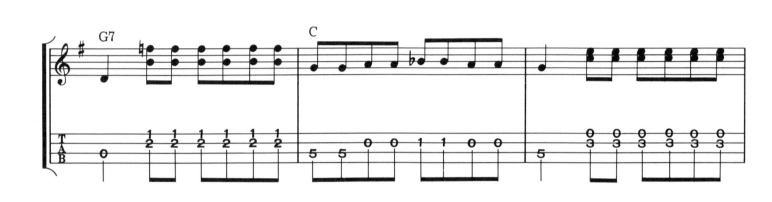

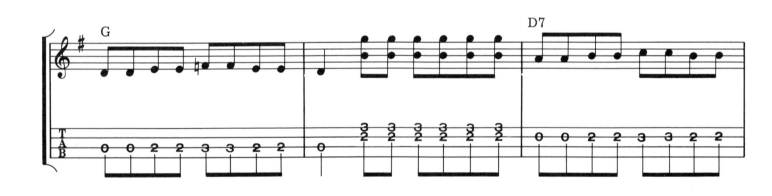

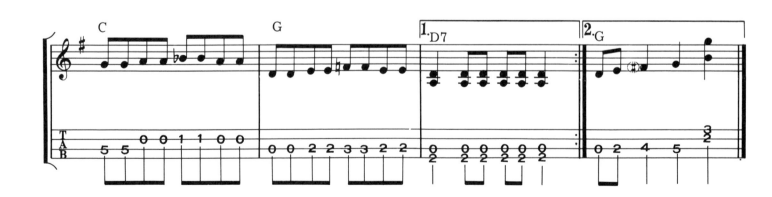

'TATER BUGGIN'

Bud Orr

MANDOLIN CAPERS

Bud Orr

DEAD END

Bud Orr

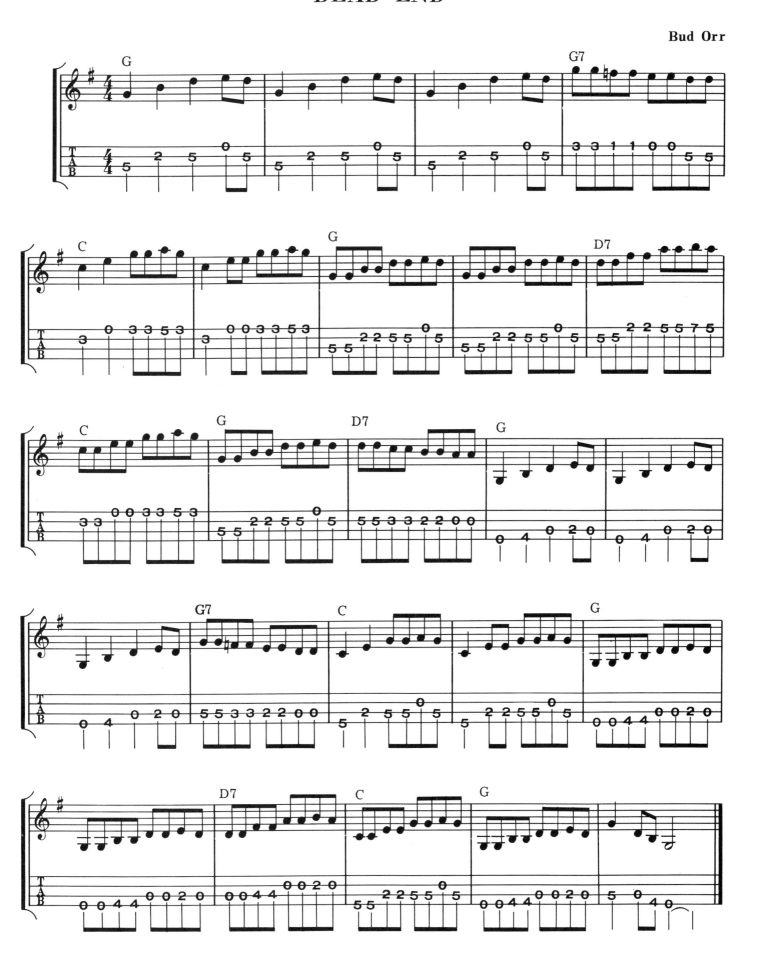

ROCK ON!

Bud Orr

MIDNITE ROCK

Bud Orr

ROCK AND BLUES RHYTHM PATTERNS
(These Patterns May Also Be Used for Lead)

Pattern Number One

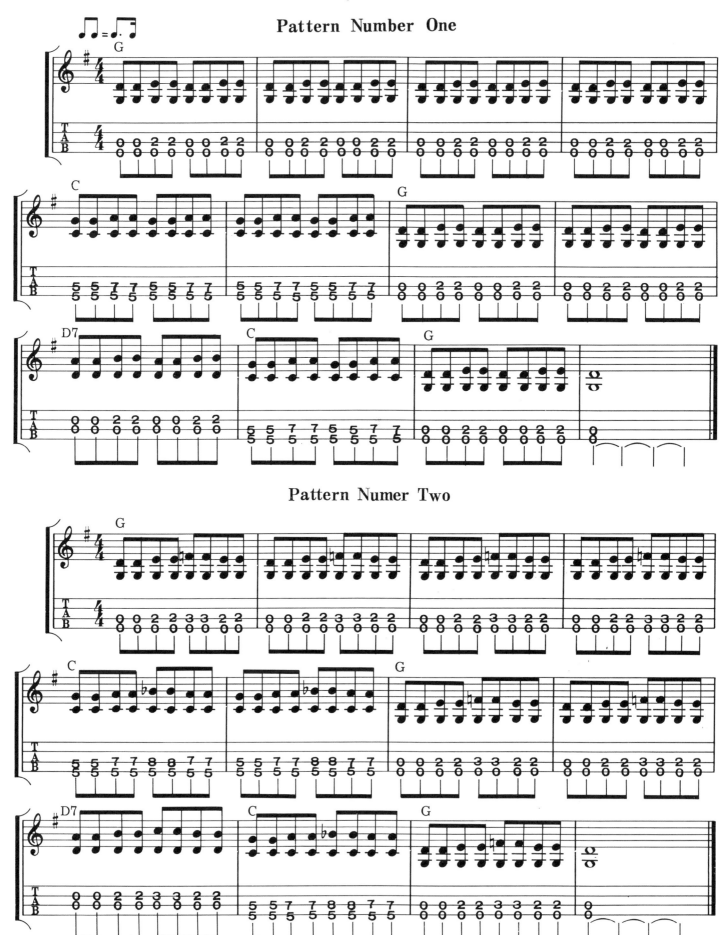

Pattern Numer Two

Pattern Number Three

Pattern Numer Four

MOVABLE ROCK AND BLUES RHYTHM PATTERNS
(With Tonic or Root Chord Note on the 4th String)

Examples using pattern number 1

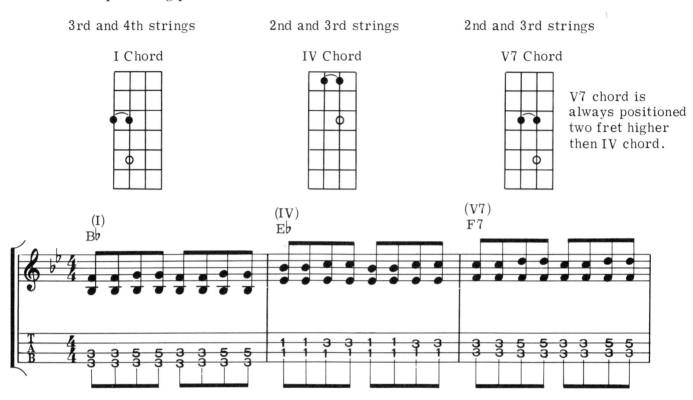

3rd and 4th strings   2nd and 3rd strings   2nd and 3rd strings

I Chord   IV Chord   V7 Chord

V7 chord is always positioned two fret higher then IV chord.

(Tonic or Root Chord Note on the 3rd String)

2nd and 3rd strings   3rd and 4th strings   3rd and 4th strings

(Two frets higher)

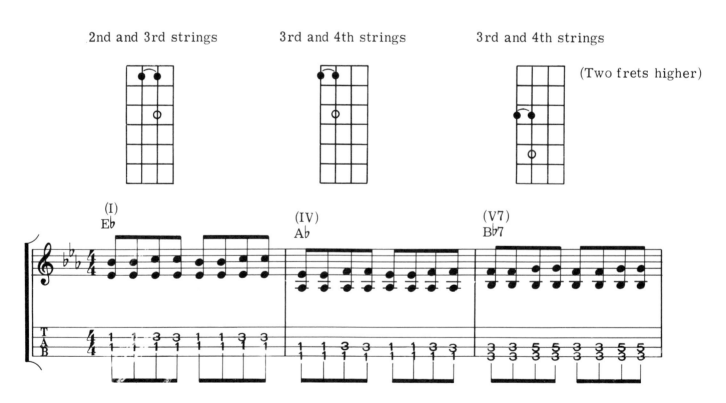

198

DIAGRAMS FOR PATTERNS 2 , 3 AND 4

(I Chord)

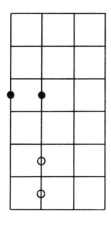

(IV Chord)

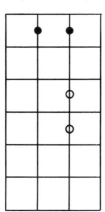

(V7 Chord)

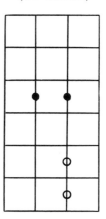

Fret	Key
1	G♯ or A♭
2	A
3	A♯ or B♭
4	B
5	C
6	C♯ or D♭
7	D
8	D♯ or E♭
9	E
10	F
11	F♯ or G♭
12	D

Fret	Key
1	D♯ or E♭
2	E
3	F
4	F♯ or G♭
5	G
6	G♯ or A♭
7	A
8	A♯ or B♭
9	B
10	C
11	C♯ or D♭
12	D

Reminder:

V7 chord is always

positioned two frets

higher than the IV

chord.

ROCK AND BLUES SCALE STUDY

The rock and blues scale consists of only five notes taken from the major scale of the same name. As shown in the example below, a rock and blues scale is derived by using the 1st., flatted 3rd, 4th, 5th and the flatted 7th of the major scale omitting the 2nd, and 6th notes.

Scale tones	1	2	3	4	5	6	7	8
G major scale	G	A	B	C	D	E	F♯	G
G rock and blues scale	G		B♭	C	D		F	G

G major scale

G rock and blues scale

200

MOVABLE ROCK AND BLUES SCALES

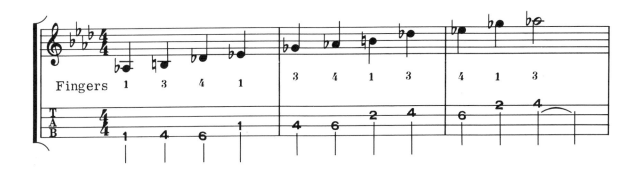

Sequence of notes		

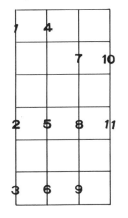

Fret	Key
1	G# or A♭
2	A
3	A# or B♭
4	B
5	C
6	C# or D♭
7	D
8	D# or E♭
9	E
10	F
11	F# or G♭
12	G

Fingers

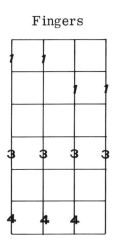

IMPROVISING WITH THE ROCK AND BLUES SCALE

Improvising (making up) a lead chorus is so simple to do that it is almost impossible to play a note that sounds wrong. Any sequence of notes will work as long as they are taken from this scale. A rock and blues chorus usually consists of 12 measures and either 3 or 4 chords. In the key of G major the chords would be; G G7 C and D7. The IV chord (C) could also be used as a 7th. In the example below the rock and blues scale is being used going up and down the scale. With practice you will discover that any rhythmic pattern will work great in any order.

202

ROCK AND BLUES CHORUS NUMBER I

The lead patterns shown below are examples only.
Ideas are endless. Feel free to improvise your own.

Bud Orr

ROCK AND BLUES CHORUS NUMBER 2

FILLS FOR ROCK AND BLUES

When playing only one chorus of rock and blues it is best to end the 12th or final measure with the root or key note. If the chorus is to be repeated one or more times a fill should be used in the repeat measure. This is always the 5th or dominant tone of the major scale.

Four Single Note Fills

Four Double Note Fills

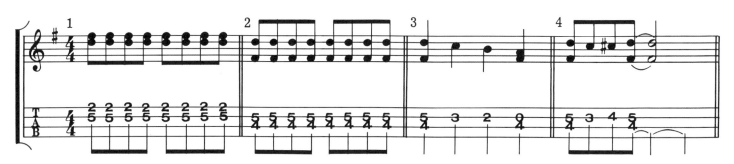

ROCK AND BLUES CHORUSES

The examples below may be used for any rhythm or lead pattern desired.

1st Rock and Blues Chorus

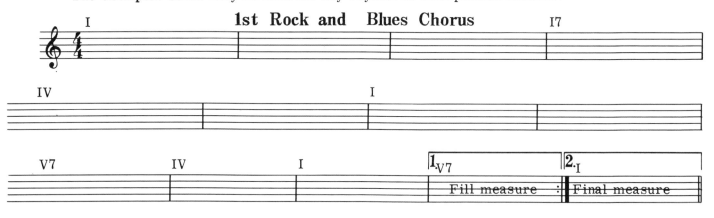

2nd Rock and Blues Chorus

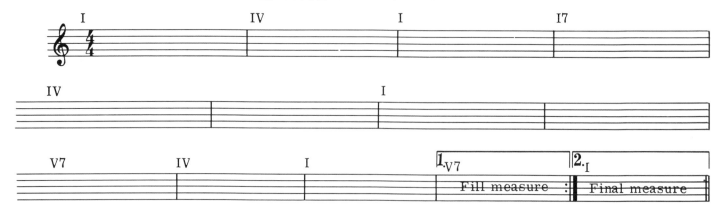

GOING STRONG

Bud Orr

Key of G
No sharp indicated

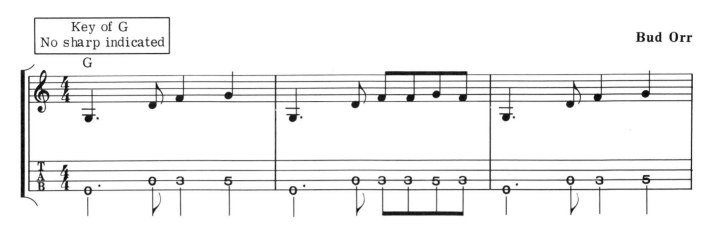

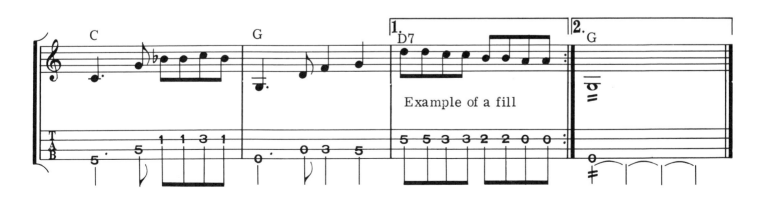

Example of a fill

MANDOLIN-OLOGY

Bud Orr

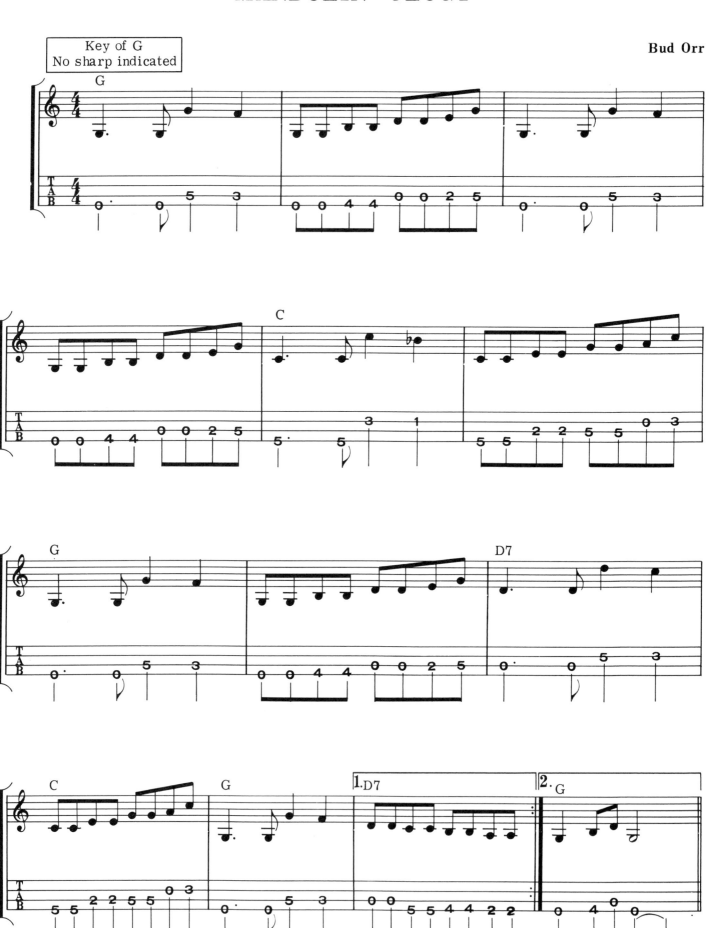

AFTER HOURS

Bud Orr

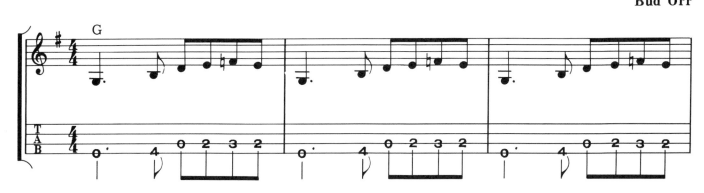

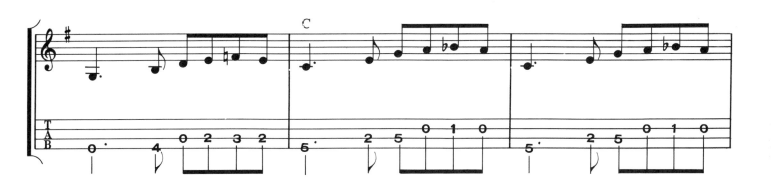

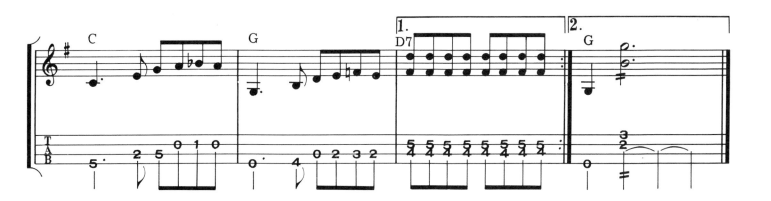

WORKING OUT

Bud Orr

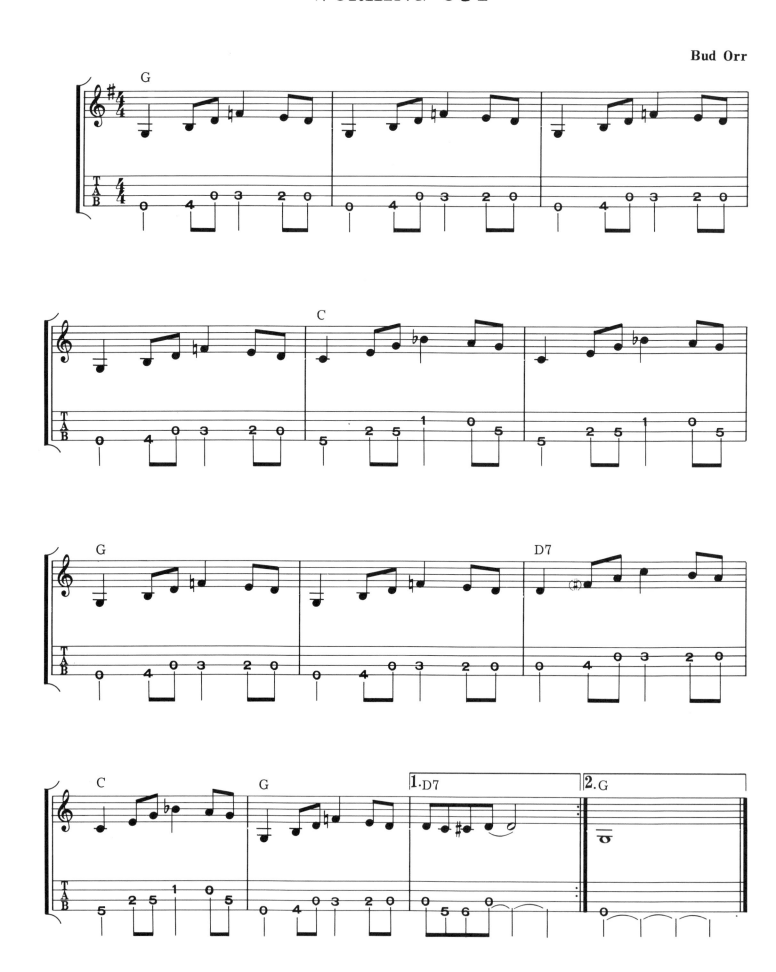

MANDOLIN BOOGIE
(Played in 2 Keys G C）

Bud Orr

THESE AWFUL BLUES

Bud Orr

Feel-in' sad and lone-ly from my head down to my shoes, Oh
Lord feel-in' sad and lone-ly from my head down to my
shoes 'cause my ba-bies gone and left me,
Left me with these aw — ful blues.

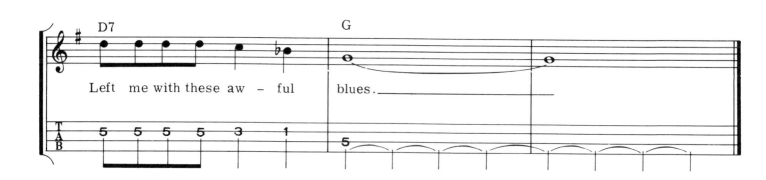

Goin' to the river with my good old rockin' chair, oh Lord. Goin' to the river with my good old rockin' chair. If these awful blues don't leave me, gonna rock a way from here.

HYMN AND GOSPEL SONG SECTION

*NO COLLECTION OF MANDOLIN MUSIC WOULD BE
COMPLETE WITHOUT SONGS OF INSPIRATION
BECAUSE THE INSTRUMENT ADAPTS TO THEM SO WELL.*

*INCLUDED IN THE FOLLOWING PAGES ARE A SELECT
GROUP OF THE MOST BELOVED HYMNS AND GOSPEL SONGS.*

PSALM 150 : 4
. . . praise him with
stringed instruments . . .

IN THE SWEET BY AND BY

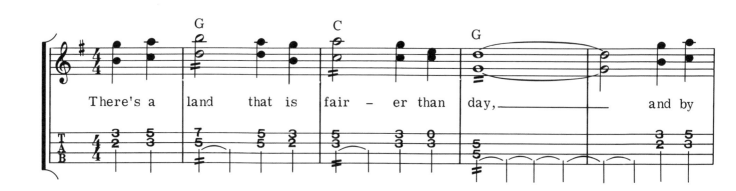

There's a land that is fair - er than day, _____ and by

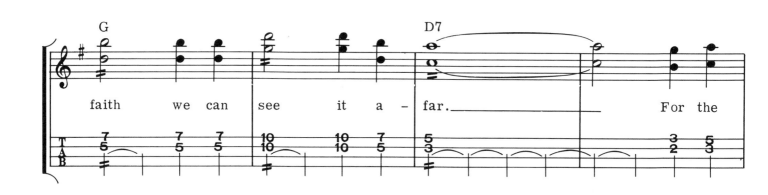

faith we can see it a - far. _____ For the

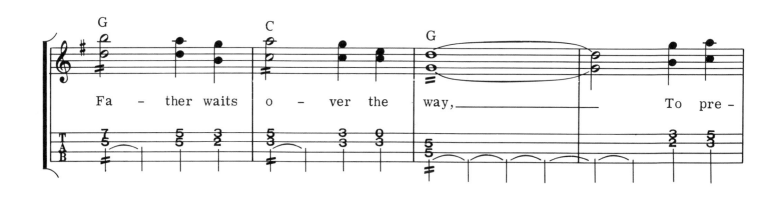

Fa - ther waits o - ver the way, _____ To pre -

pare us a dwell - ing place there. In the

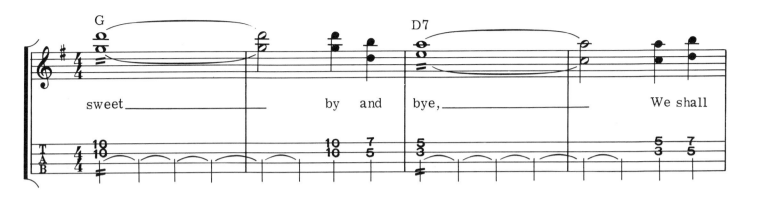

sweet_____ by and bye,_____ We shall

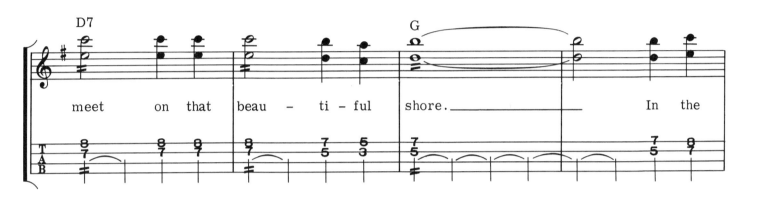

meet on that beau – ti – ful shore._____ In the

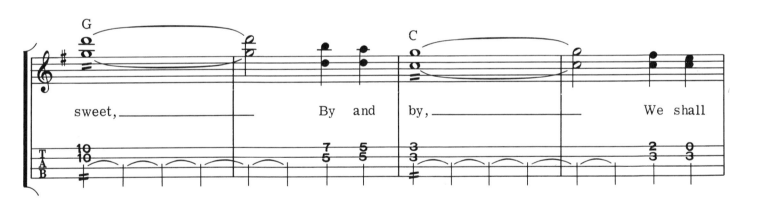

sweet,_____ By and by,_____ We shall

meet on that beau – ti – ful shore.

PASS ME NOT

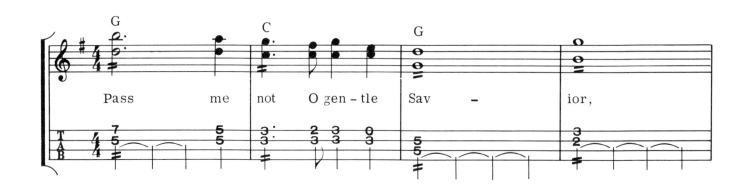

Pass me not O gen – tle Sav – ior,

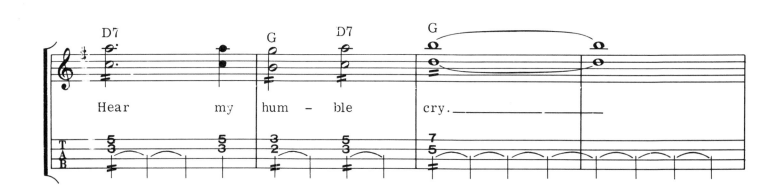

Hear my hum – ble cry._____

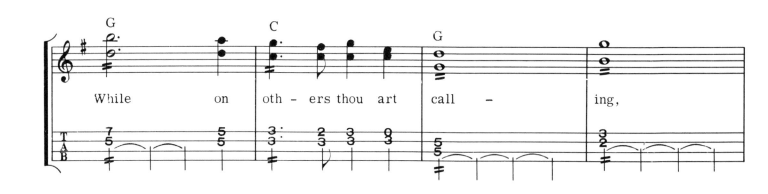

While on oth – ers thou art call – ing,

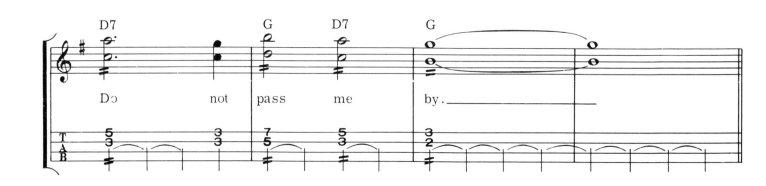

Do not pass me by._____

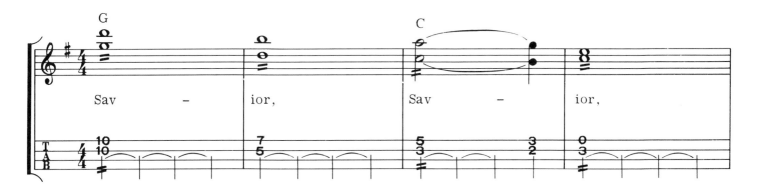

Sav - ior, Sav - ior,

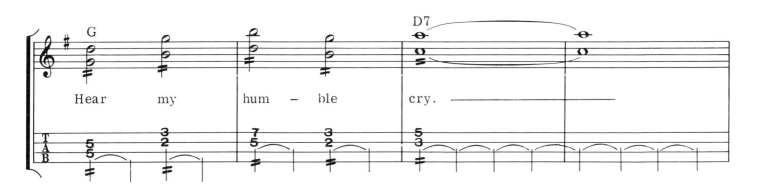

Hear my hum - ble cry. _____

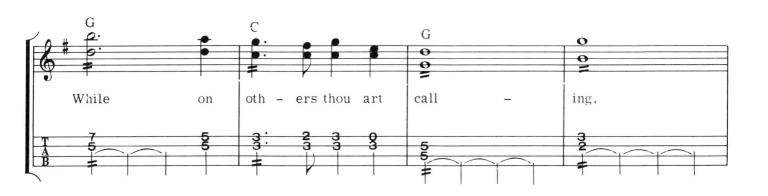

While on oth - ers thou art call - ing,

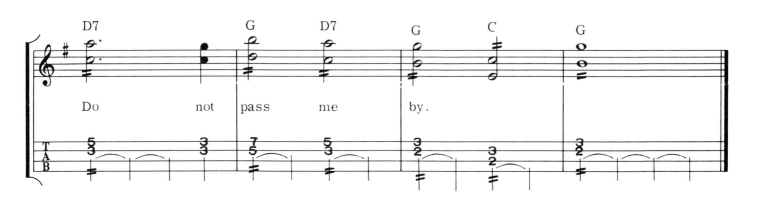

Do not pass me by.

WHO AT MY DOOR IS STANDING?

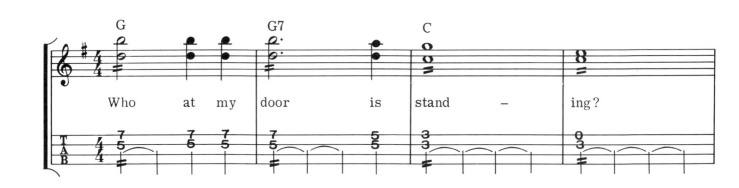

Who at my door is stand — ing?

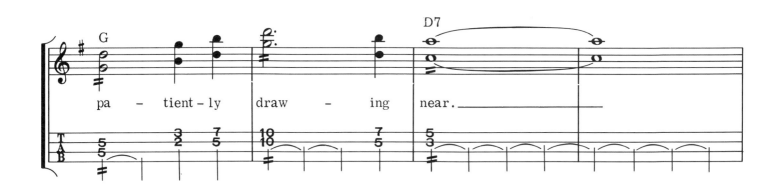

pa — tient — ly draw — ing near.

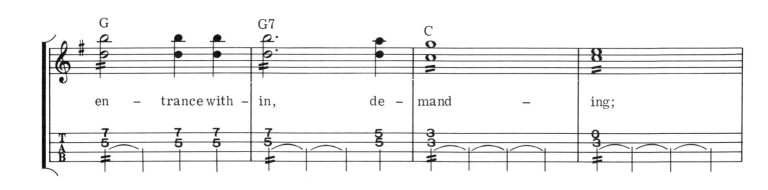

en — trance with — in, de — mand — ing;

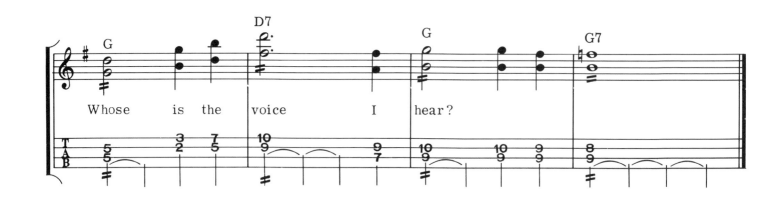

Whose is the voice I hear?

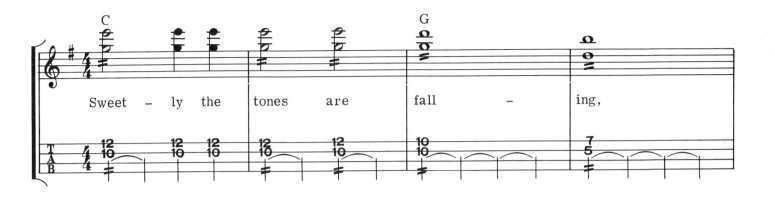

Sweet – ly the tones are fall – ing,

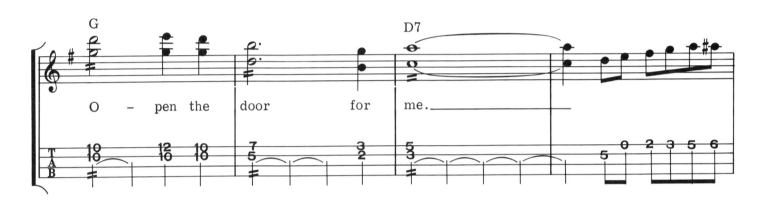

O – pen the door for me.___

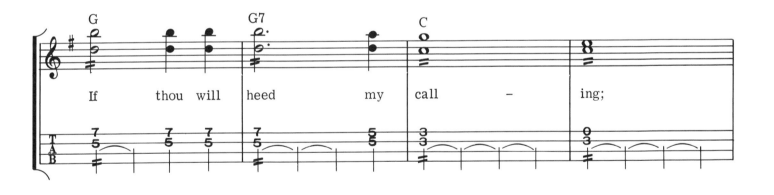

If thou will heed my call – ing;

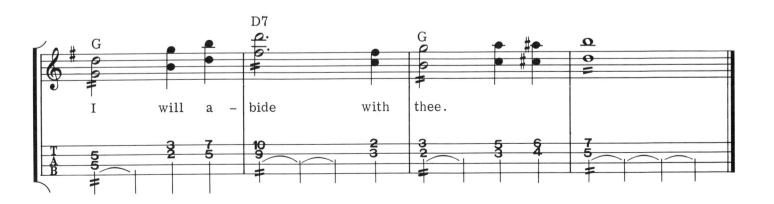

I will a – bide with thee.

WHISPERING HOPE

PRECIOUS MEMORIES

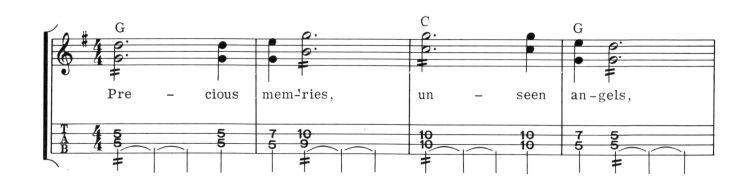

Pre — cious mem-'ries, un — seen an-gels,

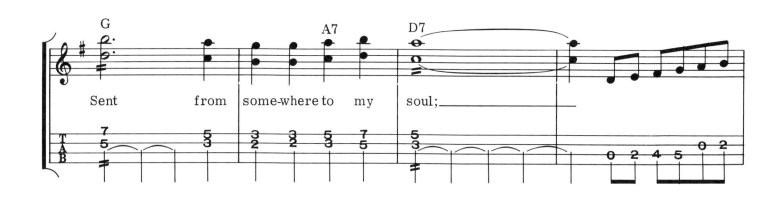

Sent from some-where to my soul;

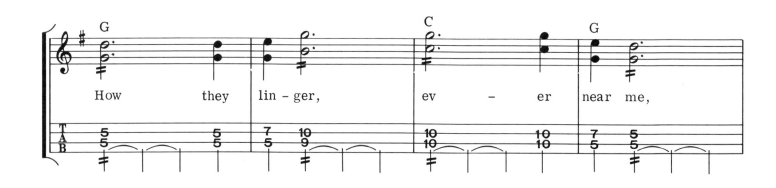

How they lin-ger, ev — er near me,

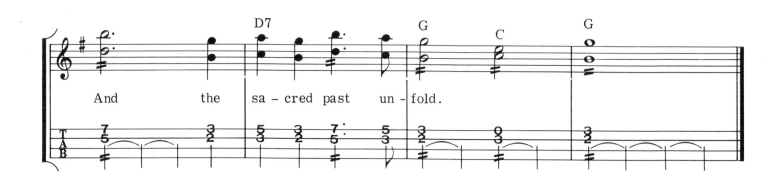

And the sa-cred past un-fold.

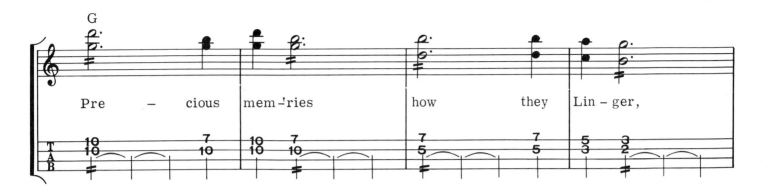

Pre — cious mem-'ries   how   they   Lin – ger,

How   they   ev – er   flood my   soul;

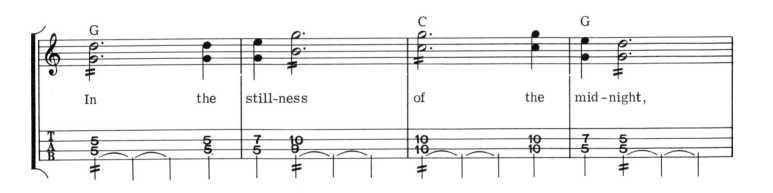

In   the   still-ness   of   the   mid –night,

Pre — cious   sa – cred scenes   un –fold.

MANDOLIN DISCOGRAPHY

The record albums contained in this discography are primarily instrumental with the exception of the Monroe Brothers and Blue Sky Boy's. These feature mandolin intros and lead breaks and are excellent examples of early country mandolin playing.

Many of the songs contained in this book are on these recordings. The arrangements are different in many ways, providing a source of listening and making up your own versions.

There are numerous fiddle, tenor banjo, flatpicking guitar, dulcimer, Greek and Irish bouzouki records available with many techniques and ideas for the mandolinist.

Classical :
The Virtuoso Classical Mandolin . . . . Everest 3244
Music For Mandolin - Beethoven - Schlick . . . . Turnabout TV 34110S
Music For Mandolin And Guitar Ensemble . . . . Turnabout TV 34239
Vivaldi - Two Concertos For Mandolin . . . . Odyssey 32-16- 0138
Vivaldi - Lute And Mandolin Concerti . . . . Turnabout TV 341532
Mandolin Music - Beethoven - Hummell . . . . Nonesuch H-71227
Music For Guitar, Lute And Mandolin . . . . Murray Hill S4757 (6 Records)

International :
Mandolins Of Sorrento . . . . Fiesta FLP 1334
The Beautiful Sound Of Neapolitan Mandolins . . . . Peters PILPS 4117
Mandolins In Italy . . . . Fiesta FLPS 1759
Encore Mandolins In Italy . . . . Fiesta FLPS 1842
Howard Frye - Gypsy Mandolin . . . . Monitor MFS 463
Dave Apollon - Mandolin Virtuoso . . . . Yazoo 1066
Cass Weir - Mandolin Magic . . . . Anet 6062N7

Jazz :
Jethro Burns - Jethro Burns . . . . Flying Fish FF 042
Jethro Burns - Live . . . . Flying Fish FF 072
Tiny Moore - Tiny Moore Music . . . . Kaleidoscope F 12
Tiny Moore - Jethro Burns - Back To Back . . . . Kaleidoscope F 9
Jethro Burns, Norman Blake, Sam Bush, Tut Taylor . . . . Flying Fish HDS 701
Jethro Burns, Others - 'S Wonderful . . . . Flying Fish FF 035
Don Stiernberg - Rosetta . . . . Flying High FH9502
Andy Statman - Flatbush Waltz . . . . Rounder Records 0116
Tim Ware - The Tim Ware Group . . . . Kaleidoscope F 13

Dawg Music : (A form of jazz played with bluegrass instruments featuring several mandolins
and related instruments.)
David Grisman - The David Grisman Quintet . . . . Kaleidoscope F 5
David Grisman - Hot Dawg . . . . Horizon SP 731
David Grisman - Quintet '80 . . . . Warner Bros BSK 3469
David Grisman - Mondo Mando . . . . Warner Bros BSK 3618
Stephane Grappelli - David Grisman - Live . . . . Warner Bros BSK 3550

Spacegrass music : (Also played with bluegrass instruments.)
The Tony Rice Unit - Mar West . . . . Rounder Records 0125
The Tony Rice Unit - Acoustics . . . . Kaleidoscope F 10
The Tony Rice Unit - Still Inside . . . . Rounder Records 0150

Early Country Mandolin (With Vocals)
Monroe Brothers - Feast Here Tonight . . . . RCA Bluebird AXM2 5510
Blue Sky Boys - 20 Country Classics . . . . RCA Camden ADL 2 0726 E

Bluegrass (including Fiddle Type tunes and Irish music)

Bill Monroe - Bill Monroe's Uncle Pen . . . . MCA DL75348
Bill Monroe - Bluegrass Instrumentals . . . . Decca DL 74601
Bill Monroe - Master Of Bluegrass . . . . MCA 5214
Kenny Baker - Kenny Baker Plays Bill Monroe . . . . County 761
          (Bill Monroe plays mandolin on this album)
Buck White - More Pretty Girls Than One . . . . Sugar Hill Records
          (SH 3710)
Bobby Osborne - Bobby Plays His Mandolin . . . . CMH Records 6256
Jesse McReynolds - Mandolin Workshop . . . . Hilltop Records
Frank Wakefield - Frank wakefield . . . . Rounder 0007
Frank Wakefield - End Of The Rainbow . . . . Bay 214
Jack Tottle - Back Road Mandolin . . . . Rounder 0067
Red Rector - Appaloosa . . . . Old Homestead 90044
Norman Blake and Red Rector . . . . County 755
Michael Melford - Mandolin Fantasy . . . . Flying Fish 023
Doyle Lawson - Tennessee Dream . . . . County 766
Jimmy Gaudreau - The Jimmy Gaudreau Mandolin Album . . . . . . Puritan 5011
Ricky Skaggs - That's It . . . . Rebel SLP 1550
Mike Lilly & Wendy Miller - New Grass Instrumentals . . . . Old Homestead 90017
Mike Lilly & Wendy Miller - Hot 'N Grassy . . . . Old Homestead 90068
Hershel Sizemore - Bounce Away . . . . County 774
Dorsey Harvey - "Dorsey Harvey" . . . . Poco River 500
Nolan Faulkner - The Legendary Kentucky Mandolin . . . . Old Homestead 90064
Jerry Stewart - Rocky Run . . . . County 767
Gus Ingo - Mandolin Album . . . . Heritage HR 20
Randy Carrier - Mandolin Picking Carrier Style . . . . Atteiram APIL 1531
Jethro Burns - Down Yonder Featuring Wade Ray . . . . RCA Camden CAS2145
Bob Clark - One Legged Gypsy . . . . Ridge Runner RRR 0025
Rick Allred & Kenneth Berrier - Fire on the mountain . . . . Old Homestead OHS 90125
Bob Dalsemer - Dick Staber - Pickin' Around The Cookstove . . . . Rounder 0040
Curley Lambert - "Bluegrass Evergreen" . . . . Old Homestead OHS 90072
Alan Munde & Sam Bush - Together again for the first time . . . . . Ridge Runner (RRR 0007)
Mick Moloney - Strings Attached . . . . Green Linnet SIF 1027
Mick Larie - La Mandoline Americaine - (French Import)
        (Bluegrass Instrumentals) Le Chant Du Monde LDX 74618
Kenny Hall - "Kenny Hall" . . . . Philo 1008

Rags Swing and Dixieland:

Dave Martini - Mr. Mandolin man . . . . Stoneway STY 126
Dave Martini - Mr. Mandolin Man Picks Again . . . . Stoneway STY 134
Dave Martini - Sounds Of The Mandolin Man . . . . Stoneway STY 174
Paul Buskirk - Hot Pickin' . . . . Stoneway STY 153

Blues :

Yank Rachell - Mandolin Blues . . . . Delmark 606

Instructional : (Very good listening albums)

Ray Valla - Bluegrass Mandolin Method . . . . Sunny Mountain Records
      Matching Record for Mel Bay Book   (EB 1002)
Robert Bolin - Twin Mandolin Workshop . . . . Workshop Records WR 1005
Michael Holmes - Old Time Country and fiddle tunes . . . . Folkways CRB 16
Greg Root - Bluegrass Mandolin . . . . Music Minus One MMO 188